40 Things to Give up for Lent and Beyond

A 40 DAY DEVOTIONAL STUDY FOR LENT

PHIL RESSLER

ISBN-13: 978-1507566213
ISBN-10: 1507566212

Dedication

To my wife Barbara.
Thank you for your continued love and support.

ACKNOWLEDGMENTS..7

INTRODUCTION...8

1. GIVING UP
FEAR OF FAILURE..11

2. GIVING UP YOUR COMFORT ZONE 14

3. GIVING UP FEELINGS OF UNWORTHINESS......................17

4. GIVING UP IMPATIENCE...20

5. GIVING UP RETIREMENT...23

6. GIVING UP
PEOPLE PLEASING...27

7. GIVING UP COMPARISON 30

8. GIVING UP BLAME..33

9. GIVING UP GUILT 36

10. GIVING UP OVERCOMMITMENT 39

11. GIVING UP
LACK OF COUNSEL 42

12. GIVING UP IMPURITY..46

13. GIVING UP ENTITLEMENT..49

14. GIVING UP APATHY 52

15. GIVING UP HATRED...55

16. GIVING UP NEGATIVITY...58

17. GIVING UP THE SPIRIT OF POVERTY 61

18. GIVING UP GOING THROUGH THE MOTIONS...............64

19. GIVING UP COMPLAINT 68

20. GIVING UP THE PURSUIT OF HAPPINESS......................71

21. GIVING UP BITTERNESS...74

22. GIVING UP DISTRACTION 77

23. GIVING UP GIVING UP 80

24. GIVING UP MEDIOCRITY...83

25. GIVING UP DESTRUCTIVE SPEECH 86

26. GIVING UP BUSYNESS 89

27. GIVING UP LONELINESS 92

28. GIVING UP DISUNITY 95

29. GIVING UP
THE QUICK FIX 98

30. GIVING UP WORRY...101

31. GIVING UP IDOLIZING 104

32. GIVING UP RESISTANCE TO CHANGE.................................107

33. GIVING UP PRIDE 110

34. GIVING UP
A SMALL VIEW OF GOD...113

35. GIVING UP ENVY...116

36. GIVING UP UNGRATEFULNESS 119

37. GIVING UP SELFISH AMBITION.................................122

38. GIVING UP SELF-SUFFICIENCY 126

39. GIVING UP SORROW...129

40. GIVING UP MY LIFE...132

CONCLUSION 135

ACKNOWLEDGMENTS

Thank you to the members of

Lutheran Church of the Good Shepherd in Old Bridge, NJ
Lord of Life Lutheran Church in LaFox, IL
and Bethany-Trinity Lutheran Church in Waynesboro, VA.

I am blessed to have been called pastor at each of these churches.
They each hold a special place in my heart. I thank each of them for
helping mold me into the pastor I am today.

INTRODUCTION

It is a tradition during the season of Lent for many people to "give something up." You may practice this tradition yourself. Some examples of the things people give up include chocolate, alcohol, smoking, television, and Facebook. There are many different reasons people give something up. As with many practices, there are some good reasons to do it and then there are some not-so-good reasons to do it.

Reasons Not to Give Something Up

Because it's tradition

There are many good traditions in the church. Most every tradition is begun for a good reason. But there often comes a time when we lose the connection with the purpose of the tradition and we continue the tradition for the sake of the tradition. If you are not sure what the purpose of the tradition is, then it may be time to stop the tradition or at the least go back and re-examine the origins.

It helps me relate to the suffering of Jesus

Many believe that making a sacrifice will help them better relate to the sufferings of Jesus. But if you think this through, does giving up Facebook for Lent even begin to come close to helping you relate to the suffering Jesus went through? We are totally missing the point. Jesus gave his life as a sacrifice. His suffering was brutal. The idea of giving up 1st world luxuries to help us relate to his suffering is laughable at best and mockery at worst.

To help me feel better about myself

Giving something up for Lent may seem like a good way to kick a bad habit. Lent may be seen as a catalyst for living a healthier and more balanced life. It might serve to help you eat better or make better use of your time. All that is commendable and God wants us to be good stewards of our lives. But this still falls short of the fuller Lenten experience.

So what is the point? Why would I give something up for Lent?

The whole idea behind giving something up is called FASTING. Fasting is a spiritual discipline much like prayer, Bible reading, and worship. In the Sermon on the Mount Jesus said, "when you fast …" He didn't say, "if you fast …" There was an expectation his followers would fast. But it is an often overlooked discipline in the church. And because we don't often teach about it, there is great misunderstanding about it.

Reasons to Give Something Up

More of God

While the idea of fasting involves taking something away, it is ultimately about more of God. Fasting, in its purest form, involves foregoing food for a certain period of time. This will lead to a hunger in our stomach which has an ultimate purpose of connecting us with our hunger for God. The time you might have spent preparing a meal and eating the meal can now be spent feasting on God's Word. In other words, spend the time you would have spent eating by reading the Bible and praying. Jesus say's, "man does not live by bread alone, but by every word that proceeds from the mouth of God" (Matthew 4:4). We realize our food and everything else we have comes from God. If God did not provide it, we would not have it (see John 6:68–69). We eliminate that which we think we need for that which we truly need.

Removing barriers

Another important aspect of fasting is cutting out that which is hindering our relationship with God. There is nothing more important in this world than our relationship with him. Yet, we allow so many other things to get in the way. Jesus say's "if your eye causes you to sin, pluck it out. If your hand causes you to sin, cut it off" (Matthew 5:29–30). The principle applies here in that we eliminate that which separates us from God. There are many things in life we think we cannot do without, but Jesus says only one thing is needful (Matthew 10:41–42).

Re-centering

Finally, fasting has a way of centering us and reminding us what is most important. We have many competing priorities in life. We don't fast for God's sake. It is a discipline given to us for our benefit. Fasting points us to what is most important. It helps us to keep the first things first. This is why we see the early church enter a time of fasting prior to making a big decisions (see Acts 13:2–3; 14:23). Fasting helps us better discern God's priorities for life and ministry.

So how about you? What are some of the reasons you fast or "give something up" during Lent? In this devotional series, we will explore 40 things worth giving up. These are things not only worth giving up during the season of Lent, but are worth giving up for the rest of your life.

1. GIVING UP FEAR OF FAILURE
ASH WEDNESDAY

Scripture Verses:

- Psalm 23
- Matthew 28:19–20
- John 14:16–17

Questions to consider:

- What is your favorite part of Lent?
- What are you afraid to start?
- If you took a step of faith into something new, what is the worst that could happen?
- How does Jesus help you overcome your fear?
- How will you pursue the presence of God this Lent?

Plan of Action:

Make a commitment for the next 40 days to confront a fear and take a step towards a calling you have been afraid to live out. Put your commitment in writing and share it with another person.

Reflection

Joshua takes over command for Moses. He had big shoes to fill. Would he be up to the task? No one would blame him for being afraid.

The first thing God says to him is:

"Be strong and courageous. Do not be frightened, and do not be dismayed, for the LORD your God is with you wherever you go." Joshua 1:9 (ESV)

It's the assigning of a new mission and the first thing God does is offer encouragement to be courageous in the face of fear. The hardest part is often starting.

We continually walk between faith and fear. These might seem mutually exclusive. But the reality is there is no faith without fear. Faith is taking that first step in spite of our fear. It is taking the leap knowing there is a chance we might fall.

The genesis of 40 Things to Give up for Lent was a commitment I made to write on my blog everyday for the 40 Days of Lent in 2014. It was fear holding me back. The writing is the easy part. The hard part is sharing. What if people don't care or like what I have to say? Certainly there are other people who are better writers and have more worthwhile stuff to share. I had a hundred different excuses not to start. But I just started writing and sharing. A couple of days later, I shared 20 Things to Give up for Lent. It went viral on the internet. Because of the response to that original post, I began to write this 40 day devotional. None of this would have happened without taking that first step. The first step is the hardest. When you take that step, God opens amazing doors.

In the end, I hope this devotion is not so much about giving something up, but stepping into a greater calling. It is setting aside the fear of failure to grab hold of God's calling on your life. Nothing worth doing will ever be easy. The best things are often the hardest things and the most fearful things.

It goes back to Jesus. Maybe that is why I love Lent so much. Lent for me is about the pursuit of God. It is the assurance of God's presence that gives us confidence. In him we find the courage to overcome our fear of failure and to take the leap into this brave new world. The more we grasp the presence of God, the more we will have the courage to overcome our fears. When we go back to the words to Joshua, the reason to not be afraid is because God is with us wherever we go. Discover him and give up your fear.

2. GIVING UP YOUR COMFORT ZONE
THURSDAY AFTER ASH WEDNESDAY

Scripture Verses

- Matthew 8:18–20
- 2 Corinthians 4:7–12

Questions to Consider

- What is something in your life you desire to change?
- What are some of your comfort zones that keep you from making the desired change?
- What are some steps you might take to move beyond those comfort zones?
- How does Jesus help us move beyond our comfort zones?

Plan of Action

Try a new experience. Examples of things you might might do:

- Try a new restaurant (if that is too much out of your comfort zone, try something different at your favorite restaurant).
- Drive a different way home from work.
- Volunteer in a new way with your church or with another community organization.
- Introduce yourself to a person you don't know. Make a new friend with someone who may look different, talk different, or think different. Learn who they are and not who you think they are.
- Just do something that is not typically you.

Reflection

Have you seen the picture above? I am not sure where it originates. I have seen it making its way around the Internet. The message is simple. The point is clear. Not much is going to change until we move out of our routine.

The cliched definition of insanity is doing the same thing over and over and expecting different results. But moving past what is comfortable is often difficult. We like the familiar and what we know. While many of us love the "idea" of change, what we don't love as much is change itself. We have a way of settling in with familiar patterns.

After the Israelites were freed from their slavery in the Old Testament, they were left to wander in the desert for 40 years. The idea of their freedom sounded great while still in Egypt, but after a short time into their journey for freedom, they wanted to turn around and go back. Had they forgotten how bad off they had it? Were they not up for this new experience in front of them?

> *And the whole congregation of the people of Israel*
> *grumbled against Moses and Aaron in the wilderness, and*
> *the people of Israel said to them, "Would that we had died*
> *by the hand of the LORD in the land of Egypt, when we sat*
> *by the meat pots and ate bread to the full, for you have*
> *brought us out into this wilderness to kill this whole*
> *assembly with hunger." Exodus 16:2–3 (ESV)*

There was no going back. After 40 years of living in the desert they entered into the Promised Land. But entering the Promised Land meant stepping out of what they knew in Egypt. It might seem like it would have been easy to leave Egypt and their slavery behind. They certainly did not love Egypt, but Egypt was what they knew.

What is your Egypt? What do you need to leave behind? What comfort zone are you holding on to which you don't want to let go? You don't love it. But it's what you know. That is why it's hard to let go.

Let's start getting comfortable with the uncomfortable. It's where the magic happens. It's where God is experienced in new ways. It's where life is lived to the fullest and joy is experienced on the journey.

When we encounter the Jesus of the Bible our comfort zone will be challenged. Jesus is all about new experiences outside our comfort zones. He called Peter out of the boat (Matthew 14:28–31). He asked the Rich Young Man to give up all his wealth (Matthew 19:21–22). He went against the status quo and challenged the religious establishment of his day (Matthew 23:1–36). Foxes have holes, and birds have nests, but the Son of Man has no place to lay his head (Luke 9:57–58).

Jesus does things differently. He has a way of helping us see things with new eyes. The truth is there is no going back to Egypt. The question is whether we will embrace the journey to the Promised Land. The more we let Jesus be our guide, the sweeter the journey becomes.

3. GIVING UP FEELINGS OF UNWORTHINESS
FRIDAY AFTER ASH WEDNESDAY

Scripture Verses

- Matthew 6:25–26
- Psalm 139:1–16
- 1 Peter 2:4–11

Questions to Consider

- In what ways do you feel inadequate or unworthy?
- What voices are you listening to which cause you to feel unworthy that you need to silence?
- What voices do you need to start amplifying?
- What does God say about your feelings of unworthiness?

Plan of Action

- If you have feelings of inadequacy or unworthiness, write a love letter to yourself. Tell yourself how much God loves you and how much you mean to him.
- Find a Bible Reading Plan. You can download our Bible Reading Plan at gs4nj.org/biblereadings. Keep in the mind that the Bible is how we hear God speak to us. In the Bible, he tells us how much he loves us and how proud he is of us.
- If you are a parent, make sure to tell your child how proud you are of them. Assure them that you love them for no other reason than the fact that they are your child. Assure them that no matter what mistakes they may make, you will always love them. This is how your Heavenly Father loves you.

Reflection

A child needs the affirmation of their father. But many times that affirmation is not there. The father may be absent or it may be that their father never told them how proud he was of them. He was quick to criticize, but slow to affirm.

When that child grows older, they will continue to search for the blessing of their father. They may become a work-a-holic, believing that through accomplishment they can finally find the fulfillment they are looking for. But they continue to live with a void. In another scenario, it might happen that feelings of unworthiness and self-doubt would be so pervasive that they never pursue God's calling on their life and settle for less.

Maybe you can relate. You desire love, respect, acceptance, or approval. But you don't feel worthy. You believe you are not accomplished enough. You believe you are not beautiful enough. You believe you are not able enough. You believe you are not _____ (You fill in the blank).

But these are lies that come straight out of the pit of hell. You are worthy enough because Jesus died for you. He accomplished everything that needed to be accomplished. He makes you beautiful. His Holy Spirit gives you the ability to accomplish all things (see Philippians 4:13).

Before Jesus began his ministry, he was baptized by John the Baptist in the Jordan River. And when Jesus was baptized, the voice of the Heavenly Father spoke from heaven:

> ***"This is my beloved Son, with whom I am well pleased."***
> ***Matthew 3:17 (ESV)***

The ministry of Jesus had yet to begin. He had not yet healed anyone. He had not yet preached any sermons of note. He had not accomplished anything worthy to be recorded in the Scriptures. But still the Father expresses his approval.

Why? It was because of the relationship of the Father to the Son. The Father's love and approval of the Son was not based on accomplishment. He loved the Son for no other reason than the fact that he was his son.

You are so important to your Heavenly Father that he sent Jesus for you. The Heavenly Father made you and created you. He gave you your life and your being. He loved you so much that he sent Jesus to die on the cross for you. It is not about anything you have accomplished. You need to know that you are the most beautiful, the most precious, and the most prized part of his creation. Your Heavenly Father is proud of you. More than you realize! You are worthy because you are his precious child, redeemed by the blood of Jesus.

We believe God expresses his love through the Bible and through Holy Communion. If the Bible is God's love letter, then Holy Communion is his hug. So I want to encourage you this Sunday, if your church is celebrating Holy Communion, to go and receive a hug from God. You may need it more than you realize.

4. GIVING UP IMPATIENCE
SATURDAY AFTER ASH WEDNESDAY

Scripture Verses

- Psalm 90:1–17
- Galatians 5:22–24
- Ephesians 4:2
- James 1:19–20

Questions to Consider

- What are you impatient about? What are some things that cause you impatience?
- What are some things that help you to relax and find peace in a busy and hurried world?
- What are some ways that you can intentionally practice patience today?
- What does Jesus teach us about patience and peace?

Plan of Action

- The next time you are at a busy store, pick the longest line. As you stand in the line, pray for the people around you. Pray that God would give them peace and patience.
- On your drive home from work, intentionally get in the slow lane. Listen to some inspirational music or an inspiration audiobook. Savor the moment. Thank God for this day. Thank him for the car you are driving. Consider how amazing is our modern day ability to travel and commute. Live in the moment.
- Be still and know God.

Reflection

Someone once told me a joke that went along these lines:

> *There was a man who once asked God, "How long is a million years to you?"*
>
> *God said, "A million years is like a second."*
>
> *Then the man said, "How much is a million dollars to you?"*
>
> *God said, "A million dollars is like a penny."*
>
> *The man smiled and said, "Could you spare a penny?"*
>
> *God smiled back and said, "Sure, just wait a second."*

God sees time very different than us. Throughout the Scriptures, it seems God seeks to teach his people lessons in patience. It was 40 years that his people wandered in the desert. It was 4000 years from the time of the fall in the Garden until the time of the Messiah. And now we are 2000 years waiting for the return of Christ. But everything happens in God's good timing.

I want you to consider 3 aspects of patience in regards to faith and life.

Patience towards God

Patience towards God is the patience to wait for God's answer to prayer, no matter how agonizing it might be. It is always believing his time is the best time. When we find a growing impatience towards God, we can go back to the invitation in Psalm 46:10: "Be still and know that I am God."

Patience with Yourself

Patience with yourself is is to recognize that accomplished people are not born accomplished people. In 1 Timothy 4:7, the Apostle Paul says, "train yourself to be godly." Training is pushing ourselves to do what we can today so that we can do tomorrow what we can't do today. Growth is a process that takes time and does not happen overnight. Be patient with yourself. You are on the way. Don't be in a rush to get there. Enjoy the journey.

Patience towards Others

Patience towards others is difficult when we feel they have taken advantage of us, when we feel they don't listen to us, when we feel they have wronged us, or when they don't agree with us.

But the reason we can be patient with others is because God was first patient with us. Though we are sinners and do not deserve his love, he still loves us. He still waits for us and gives us the opportunity to try again. It is called forgiveness. And he doesn't just forgive us once. He forgives us over and over and over and over. In the words of Jesus, we forgive "seventy times seven." It was a fancy way of saying he forgives us to infinity (see Matthew 18:21–22).

> *The Lord is not slow to fulfill his promise as some count slowness, but is patient toward you, not wishing that any should perish, but that all should reach repentance. 2 Peter 3:9 (ESV)*

When it all comes down to it, patience is about love. Love is patient! It is the first characteristic of love described in 1 Corinthians 13:4. Being patient towards others is making it about them rather than making it about us. Impatience happens when we are focused on ourselves and our priorities. Patience happens when our focus is on God and others. Let's start looking outside ourselves!

5. GIVING UP RETIREMENT
WEEK #1 MONDAY

Scripture Verses

- Mark 10:42–45
- John 14:12–17
- Colossians 3:23–24
- Ephesians 2:10

Questions to Consider

- What are the non-monetary benefits of work?
- What are the challenges you have with work?
- What do you think God has to say about those challenges?
- What does it mean to work for the Lord and not man?
- What is the role of "the Helper" (see John 14:16) in your work?

Plan of Action

- Bless someone in an unexpected way today. You might: Write a thank you note. Treat someone to lunch or coffee. Volunteer for a menial task which others are reluctant to raise their hand.
- Write down things you are passionate about doing. It could be anything. Then consider how you might use these passions to serve God and others.

Reflection

Happy Monday. It is the beginning of a new work week and today we are giving up retirement. It may not be what you think. You may retire from your career, but if you are still breathing, you are here for a purpose. God is not finished with you yet. There is work for you to do.

WORK is often viewed as a four letter word. It is seen as a bad thing. But when God created man, he created him to work and tend the Garden of Eden. Work was good. Work gave Adam a purpose and a mission.

> *The LORD God took the man and put him in the Garden of Eden to work it and keep it. Genesis 2:15 (ESV)*

But what happened? When Adam and Eve fell into sin, there was a curse put over work. Work would now be hard and difficult.

> *And to Adam he said ... "cursed is the ground because of you; in pain you shall eat of it all the days of your life; thorns and thistles it shall bring forth for you; and you shall eat the plants of the field. By the sweat of your face you shall eat bread, till you return to the ground, for out of it you were taken; for you are dust, and to dust you shall return." Genesis 3:17–19 (ESV)*

Work from that point forward would be associated with toil and sweat. But apart from the curse work is a good thing. Through the cross of Jesus Christ, work is redeemed.

On earth, I see 4 different types of work:

- **Work you detest.** This is work you will do anything to get out of.

- **Work you tolerate.** This is not work you enjoy. It is a big drain, but you do it.

- **Work you enjoy.** This is work you are happy to do, but at the end of the day you have your fill.

- **Work you are passionate for.** This is work you live for. It doesn't wear you out, but fills you up.

The work you do for a paycheck falls somewhere in those four categories. Some people are blessed to have a career that falls in line with their passion. Other people may have a career where they live for the weekend. But our "career" work is not necessarily the work to define us.

I want you to separate the work you do from the paycheck you receive. There is the work of being a parent. There is the work of being a spouse. There is the work of being a leader in your church. There is the work of being a volunteer in your community. These are different vocations. We don't always get a paycheck for this work, but it is often the most fulfilling work we do.

Many people who lose their jobs fall into depression. I believe that much of that can be attributed to a loss of purpose. Remember God created us to work and to serve. We were wired that way. When we lose that part of our life, there is something missing. So make sure to remember that your work is defined by more than your career.

There are different seasons of life. And there are different callings for different times. The work we do changes over time. But we don't really retire from the work God gives us, we just transition in our calling.

Wherever you are in life, strive to find that work you are passionate about. It may be coaching your daughter's basketball team. It may be mentoring incarcerated youth. It may be playing an instrument on your church's praise team. Look to find it. The benefit of this work is not necessarily a paycheck, but in the fulfillment we find with living in line with God's purposes.

"Whatever you do, work heartily, as for the Lord and not for men, knowing that from the Lord you will receive the inheritance as your reward. You are serving the Lord Christ." Colossians 3:23–24 (ESV)

The greatest work of all is the saving work of Jesus. It certainly was not pleasant work by any stretch of the imagination. Yet, the Bible says he did this agonizing work out of joy.

"... who for the joy that was set before him endured the cross, despising the shame ... " Hebrews 12:2 (ESV)

The passion Jesus had for this most difficult work was his love for you. The joy was the vision set before him of having you in eternity forever with him. That made it all worth it. So when you find work difficult, keep your eyes on the prize. Keep your eyes on Jesus.

So how about you? What's God having you doing these days? It's time to get to work!

6. GIVING UP PEOPLE PLEASING
Week #1 Tuesday

Scripture Verses

- 2 Timothy 4:1–8
- Isaiah 8:8–13
- Luke 13:31–35

Questions to Consider

- How has your need to please people compromised your desire to please God?
- Who are the people you aim to please? Why?
- What does it mean to speak the truth in love (See Ephesians 4:15)? What is the relationship of truth to love?
- How does Jesus help us overcome our need to please people?

Plan of Action

- Our need to please often arises out of our own need for approval. Who are the people in your life who love you unconditionally? Make sure to thank them for loving you unconditionally for who you are and allowing you to be yourself.
- Minimize the voices of those you cannot make happy. Tune them out. Turn them off. There are plenty of other people out there who would benefit from what you have to offer. Jesus says, "if you are not accepted, shake the dust off your feet and move on." (Matthew 10:14)
- If you have a person you cannot make happy but can't tune them out, seek to understand their perspective. Try to put yourself in

their shoes. Look at the situation with their eyes. Be patient with them. Pray for them. Love them. But don't compromise God's plan for your life.

Reflection

Hello, my name is Phil and I am a recovering people pleaser. I am sure many of you are just like me. Many of you are continually striving for acceptance. You yearn for the affection of others. When I first became a pastor, I thought it was my role to make everyone happy. I did not want to upset or offend anyone. I wanted people to like me, but it often held me back from doing what I knew God was leading and calling me to do. It stunted the potential growth of our ministry.

You know how the cliche goes:

"You can please some of the people some of the time, but you can't please all the people all the time."

There is truth in these words. You can't make everyone happy. So stop trying. Not even Jesus made everyone happy.

Love is not always doing the thing people want you to do. That is called enabling. Love is doing for them what you believe in your heart and you know from God to be best for them.

We learn this from the prophets in the Old Testament. We learn this from Jesus himself. They did not always tell people what they wanted to hear. They told them what they needed to hear. It cost Jesus and many of the prophets their lives. Love involves sacrifice.

If you are a leader, then set the course according to where God is directing you. Certainly listen to the advice and wisdom of others. In fact, you need to do that. But make sure God is the one navigating. Not everyone is going to come along and follow. But that is ok. If God has got you on course, you need to keep looking forward.

When I worked as a counselor at Lake Wapogasset Lutheran Bible

Camp, we would take the campers canoeing. The camp was on a big lake. When crossing the lake, I would tell the campers to pick a landmark on the other side of the lake. Then I would tell them to keep their canoe pointed at that landmark. The quickest way across the lake was a straight line.

There is a danger when we value the thoughts and the opinions of others more than we value the will of God. It will hold us back from walking in the destiny he has in store for us. When we give into people pleasing, we lose our focus and direction. We will be steered in all sorts of different directions. Little progress will be made toward the destination. Find the landmark of Jesus Christ. Keep steering straight towards him.

7. GIVING UP COMPARISON
Week #1 Wednesday

Scripture Verses

- Philippians 3:4–10
- Job 40:3–41:34

Questions to Consider

- What are some ways you compare yourself to others? Why?
- What is the danger of comparing yourself to others?
- What do you base your value on?
- Why does God value you? What does that mean to you?

Plan of Action

- Make a list of accomplishments you are proud of. Thank God for giving you the skill, talent, and ability to do these things.
- Consider if there is something you are doing in your life purely for the recognition that comes along with it. Give it up. Or repurpose your ambition to serve others.
- Praise God when others are able to accomplish more than you for God's kingdom. Remember it's not about you. It's about God's work, which is bigger than any one of us.

Reflection

There is always going to be someone better, someone more accomplished, someone more beautiful, someone more blessed, someone more skilled. If you continue to compare yourself you are going to find you never match up. It will seem like you are always lacking.

I have a "type A" personality and I strive to be good at everything I do. I am competitive and I want to be the best. It puts me on this never ending quest for perfection. Nothing is ever good enough. There is always some way to improve. There is always something to tweak.

There is this twinge I get inside my stomach when I see someone excelling in a way I am not able. There is a pain inside me where I feel as if I am not measuring up. I wonder what is wrong with me and ask why can't I be like this other person.

A big reason for this is because I find my value in terms of how I am appreciated by others. I thrive on being complimented. My sin is I am making recognition by others my god. It becomes my idol. The problem is that a false god cannot provide for me in the way that Jesus provides. The love I get from this "god of recognition" is dependent upon my ability to excel.

While we want to give our best for God, there comes a time to stop. There is a time to take satisfaction in what we have done. Let God take care of the rest. Our work may not match up with the Joneses, but that is ok. We are not the Joneses and we probably don't want to be the Joneses. The Joneses are likely agonizing over comparing themselves to the Smiths.

You are created by God. You are who you are. He loves you for who you are. You don't need to be something you are not. His love is not based upon your accomplishment or your skill. You are beautiful and wonderful to him because he made you unique. You are his child.

The sooner you accept your limitations, the better off you will be. This is why the Apostle Paul writes:

"But whatever gain I had, I counted as loss for the sake of Christ." Philippians 3:7 (ESV)

As you come to the end of yourself, you discover the beginning of him. You cannot win at the game of comparison until you realize there is none like Jesus. No one can compare to him.

31

"Indeed, I count everything as loss because of the surpassing worth of knowing Christ Jesus my Lord. For his sake I have suffered the loss of all things and count them as rubbish, in order that I may gain Christ."
Philippians 3:8 (ESV)

8. GIVING UP BLAME
Week #1 Thursday

Scripture Verses

- Genesis 3:1–24
- Nehemiah 1:4–11
- Romans 8:31–39

Questions to Consider

- Who are you blaming for a certain situation or circumstance? What was your role?
- Why do we blame others for our circumstances rather than accept responsibility?
- What are some ways we own responsibility for our actions when we come to repentance?
- How does Jesus help us overcome blaming others for our hardship?

Plan of Action

- Ask for forgiveness for your part in a conflict. Be the bigger person. You might be able to win the argument, but winning the argument is not worth losing the relationship.
- If having been victimized in your past is holding back your future, seek Pastoral or Christian counseling. Seek healing for your wounds. Don't let the past actions of others rob you of your present and your future.
- Part of accepting responsibility is making restitution. This is hard. It is one thing to be sorry for your actions. It is another thing to compensate others for ways you have wronged them. Consider one way you need to make restitution with another person today and then go do it.

Reflection

It's not my fault. The devil made me do it. It goes all the way back to the Garden of Eden. It goes all the way back to the fall into sin. We blame others for our actions. Eve blamed the serpent. Adam blamed Eve (see Genesis 3:11–13). We are good at playing the victim. We are innocent. Like Pontius Pilate, we try to wash our hands clean in spite of the blood on them.

Healing relationships starts with repentance. It starts with me owning my part of the dysfunction. Rarely is one party the sole party to be blamed. Both parties have part in the conflict. It is easy to see the other person's fault. What is more difficult is to see my own fault.

This is not to say there are not innocent victims caught in abuse. There is evil in this world. Many times the darkness strikes the innocent. Many of you reading this have been victimized in the past. It has left a wound that will not heal.

You cannot control what others do to you. What you can control, with the help of the Holy Spirit, is how you respond. With the help of the Holy Spirit, you can respond in love. With the help of the Holy Spirit, you can move forward. With the help of the Holy Spirit, you can find the healing which is missing.

Letting the past actions of others control your present and your future is allowing them to victimize you all over again. When we find our identity in Christ, we cannot go back to being the victim.

> *"No, in all these things we are more than conquerors through him who loved us." Romans 8:37 (ESV)*

Through Christ Jesus, we are more than conquerors in all things. This verse does not say we are conquerors in some things. It says we are conquerors in all things. Neither does it say we are just conquerors. It says we are 'more than conquerors.'

As Jesus hung upon the cross, it would have been easy for him to blame others. It would have been easy for him to accuse those who put him there. He truly was the victim, the innocent lamb led to the slaughter (see Isaiah 53:7). His victimization could have kept him from walking in the destiny the Father had prepared for him. But his response was:

"Father, forgive them, for they know not what they do."
Luke 23:34 (ESV)

He chose to take the accusations against us upon himself. He took the blame, even though he was innocent. By his wounds we are now healed.

Know that hurting people hurt others. Hurting people often hurt themselves. But as you find healing in Jesus Christ, something amazing happens. The scars left behind become a reminder that I am not a victim but "more than a conqueror" and the wounds of the past become agents of healing.

9. GIVING UP GUILT
Week #1 Friday

Scripture

- Psalm 103:1–22
- 1 John 1:5–10
- John 3:16–18

Questions

- In what areas of life do you live with guilt?
- How is our guilt removed? What is the cost of our guilt being removed?
- What does Jesus say about your guilt?
- How do we help others overcome their guilt?

Plan of Action

- When you wake up in the morning, thank God for the new day. Thank him for new opportunities. Thank him that today is not yesterday.
- Make an appointment with your pastor to confess your sins. Allow your pastor to announce God's forgiveness over you.
- Write down your sin and guilt on a paper. Then take that paper and burn it. Remember that God makes your sins to be no more and removes them as far as the east is from the west (see Psalm 103:12).

Reflection

Today we are giving up guilt. There are three types of guilt I want to talk about. There is past, present, and future guilt.

Past Guilt

The past is the past. There is no going back. You can't change the past. You can't relive the past. Don't keep going back to the past. Today is a new day. It is the first day of the rest of your life. Jesus has redeemed your life. He has forgiven your sins. He has given you a new start.

We can learn from our past. It is said we learn from the mistakes of others. We also learn from our own mistakes. Moving forward, we may avoid past mistakes, but we don't need to live with the guilt of them. While the past may shape us and guide us, the past will not define us.

> *"Therefore, if anyone is in Christ, he is a new creation. The old has passed away; behold, the new has come."*
> *2 Corinthians 5:17 (ESV)*

Jesus came to set us free from our guilt. In him, we move forward in freedom from the guilt of the past.

Present Guilt

This is when we keep making the same mistakes over and over. This is when we don't live up to our expectations. This is when we fall short of the goals we have made. This is when we try to give up a bad habit or addiction, but cannot overcome.

Know the path to victory is never a straight line. For every two steps forward, there is one step back. As we pursue God's path, Satan will work even harder to push us off course.

Jesus enables us to keep moving forward.

> *"Therefore, since we are surrounded by so great a cloud of witnesses, let us also lay aside every weight, and sin which clings so closely, and let us run with endurance the race that is set before us." Hebrews 12:1 (ESV)*

That doesn't mean it will be easy. That does not mean it will be without setbacks. But when you can't, know that Jesus can. Ask him for his help. Seek his strength. When we receive the Lord's Supper it is not just about receiving forgiveness for past sins, but it is also receiving the presence of God in our lives to overcome present challenges.

Future Guilt

The day is coming when we will all stand before the throne of the righteous judge. We will all need to give an account of our lives on earth. At that time, we will all receive the pronouncement of guilty or not guilty.

Apart from Jesus, the only possible pronouncement is guilty. We have no answer to the charges against us. Each of us has sinned and fallen short of the glory of God (see Romans 3:23). We are guilty as charged.

But Jesus paid it all. He takes our guilt upon himself when we receive the gift of his salvation by faith. He receives the punishment that was ours. He takes our place.

Although there is nothing you deserve from God except his eternal punishment, he offers his undeserved love through Jesus Christ. We sometimes may think that we need to go back and do something more to cover our sin. But Jesus did all that was necessary. There is nothing more to be done.

When we continue to live and to persist in our guilt, we are taking away from what Jesus did for us on the cross. It is to say the cross is not enough. But we can't do anything more than Jesus has already done. And to even think we could do any more is misguided at best.

What can wash away my sin? Nothing but the blood of Jesus;
What can make me whole again? Nothing but the blood of Jesus.

Oh! precious is the flow That makes me white as snow;
No other fount I know, Nothing but the blood of Jesus.

10. GIVING UP OVERCOMMITMENT
Week #1 Saturday

Scripture Verses

- Isaiah 56:1–8
- Matthew 5:37
- Matthew 11:25–30

Questions to Consider

- In what areas of your life do you feel overcommitted and overburdened?
- Why is overcommitment bad for us and for others?
- How can you start to move your priorities towards what is truly important and leave behind those things which are less important?
- How does Jesus enable us to overcome our overcommitment?

Plan of Action

- Write down one thing God would have you accomplish today. Then make it a priority to do it. Stay focused on that one priority. Don't do anything else until you have finished.
- Consider your many commitments. It is time to purge. It is time to say no. Eliminate one commitment you have made that is taking away from your other commitments.
- Make one day this week an actual Sabbath. Don't work. Eliminate any commitments for that day.

Reflection

There are 24 hours in a day. There are 7 days in a week. There are 365 days in a year. If you believe God knows what he is doing, then you believe God created just the right amount of time. He gave you 24 hours in a day to do everything he intended you to do. If you can't do everything in 24 hours, then there is a good chance you are doing more than he ever intended for you to accomplish.

We always have enough time to do what is important to us. You make time for your priorities. When you don't get something done, it means the priority was not there.

Every time we say "yes" to one thing we are saying "no" to another thing. We try to have it all. We try to do it all. But we are finite beings with limited time. We are not God, even though we try to be.

Jesus says:

> **"Let what you say be simply 'Yes' or 'No.'"**
> **Matthew 5:37 (ESV)**

Many of us are good at saying yes. We are not as good at saying no.

The key here is to make God's priorities your priorities. One of God's priorities is for you to have margin in your life. The margin is the space in your life which is not committed to any particular thing. The problem is we are committed to the point we can't take on any more commitments. It is a situation which is unsustainable.

We need to learn to say no to the wrong things, so that we can say yes to the right things. The problem is that the wrong things are not often clear. This is where we need discernment. The discernment comes from God.

In our Lutheran tradition, the third commandment is: "Remember the Sabbath day by keeping it holy." (Exodus 20:8) The Sabbath Day is a day of rest. It was a day to stop. It was a day to create margin in our lives. One of the reasons we rush so much is because we believe everything is dependent upon us. The Sabbath Day is a way of putting our work in God's hands. It is trusting him to accomplish what we cannot accomplish.

As much as it is important to build Sabbath rest into your week, it is important to build Sabbath rest into your day. In my own personal life, there are many days I am tempted to skip my morning time of devotions and prayer. There are many days I think to myself that I don't have enough time. But I find the days when I pause to put my work in God's hands are the days I am most productive. The days I plow forward into my work without him are usually the days I end up frustrated and unproductive. The reason I believe this to be true is because by setting aside this time, I am allowing God to establish my priorities. He gives me the insight to say no to what I need to say no to and yes to what I need to say yes to.

There is a lot to do. It's time to say no, so that we can say yes to all the incredible things God has in store. Remember your value is not found in what you accomplish, but in what Jesus accomplished for you.

11. GIVING UP
LACK OF COUNSEL
Week #2 Monday

Scripture Verses

- 1 Kings 12:1–24
- 2 Timothy 3:10 - 4:5

Questions to Consider

- Who are some mentors you admire?
- Why is it important to seek the counsel of others?
- What are some of the qualities and characteristics of people who make good advisors?
- How do we seek the wisdom of God in our lives? How does God give wisdom?

Plan of Action

- Make an inventory of people you are listening to. Consider if their lives are worth emulating. Find ways to start listening to the people you admire more. Find ways to eliminate listening to the people you admire less.
- Find a mentor for a specific area of your life where you may be struggling. This is someone you may look up to or who is accomplished in a given field. Seek to learn from this person how they got to where they got. Read their book. Listen to their podcast. Call them up. Invite them to lunch.
- Consider if the life you are living is the life you would want another person to live. Make the necessary changes to live the type of life that is worth passing on to others. Share the story of your journey.

Reflection

You don't know what you don't know! You may think you know but you don't. How many of us wish we knew in our younger years what we know now? Back then, we thought we knew. However, as we have grown older, we have learned our parents were much wiser than we thought. Maybe one of the most important lessons we learn as we grow older is that we don't know it all.

This is why we are giving up "lack of counsel." One place we can seek advice and wisdom is from our peers. It is good to be a part of a community with people on a similar journey so we can share our experiences. But we should not limit seeking counsel from our peers alone.

It is easy to default to the advice of our peers. But our peers are often engaged in many of the same struggles as we are engaged in. If you are drowning in the same water as someone else, it is not much help to get advice from that person. It is much better to look to someone who has made it out of the water to help you get out. Yet we find it much easier to pool our ignorance together with our peers. The problem is we may never get beyond our present challenges.

Looking outside our group of peers may make us uncomfortable. It may stretch us. But to move beyond our current circumstances will require new ways of seeing and doing. In the Book of Proverbs it says:

> *"Without counsel plans fail, but with many advisers they succeed." Proverbs 15:22 (ESV)*

When King Rehoboam, the son of Solomon, became king in his father's place, he was confronted by the subjects of his kingdom. These subjects had suffered greatly under the rule of Solomon. They now asked Rehoboam to relent and to change the overbearing policies of his father.

When confronted with this request, Rehoboam did not turn to the experienced advisors of his father. Instead he turned to the friends of his youth who had no experience governing a kingdom. The result was devastating. When Rehoboam failed to relent, the subjects revolted. The kingdom was divided. And Rehoboam almost lost his life. (see 1 Kings 12:1–24)

If Rehoboam had listened to the counsel of his father's advisors, all that would have likely been avoided. But Rehoboam thought he knew better. He surrounded himself with people who would only tell him what he wanted to hear rather than what he needed to hear.

Part of the reason for seeking advisors is to help us discover what we don't know. When we come to know that we don't know, we are at a better place to make informed decisions. As we seek wise counselors in our life, we don't limit ourselves to the counsel of one source alone. We need to consider multiple sources to teach us. Here are a few:

- **The Scriptures** - the Apostle Paul writes: "All Scripture is breathed out by God and profitable for teaching, for reproof, for correction, and for training in righteousness, that the man of God may be complete, equipped for every good work" (2 Timothy 3:26–17 ESV).
- **Church community** - The church is not perfect. But God gives us the gift of the church to share the struggle of our journey together. It is important to have people in your life who are going to influence you towards God, rather than away from God.
- **Parents, spouses, family** - These people know us well and we are wise to listen to their counsel.
- **Books** - This is one of the easiest ways to learn from others.
- **Conferences** - There are many conferences on many different topics. One of the values of conferences is meeting other people on the journey.
- **Websites and blogs** - There are many great online communities which you can become a part of that offer help along the way.
- **Mentors** - This is one of the most valuable forms of counsel after the Scriptures. We would do well to be more intentional with mentoring relationships.

- **Prayer** - Ask God to reveal his wisdom to you. But make sure to watch for him to do that. It will usually come from one of the sources above.

So where do you need some wisdom? Is your marriage struggling? Is your work stuck in a funk? Are you having trouble connecting with God? Seek counsel and aid. If you could have figured it out on your own, you would have done so already. Don't be afraid to ask for help. It's ok! You are not expected to know it all. That is why God gives us many mentors in life.

12. GIVING UP IMPURITY
Week #2 Tuesday

Scripture Verses

- Matthew 5:27–30
- 1 Corinthians 6:12–20
- James 3:13–18

Questions to Consider

- Why does God command us to avoid sexual impurity?
- What are the consequences of sexual impurity for individuals, families, society, and the Church?
- What steps do you take to intentionally live holy and pure?
- How does Jesus help us live pure lives?

Plan of Action

- Take an inventory of media you consume. Cut out media which is less than wholesome. Replace it with something which will point you towards God rather than away from him.
- If sexual impurity is a challenge in your life, build accountability into your life.
- Be vigilant towards what your children are being exposed to. Talk with them about it. Consider how you might protect them.

Reflection

Today we cover a weighty subject. We are talking about giving up impurity. The Apostle Paul writes:

> *"Finally, brothers, whatever is true, whatever is honorable, whatever is just, whatever is pure, whatever is*

lovely, whatever is commendable, if there is any excellence, if there is anything worthy of praise, think about these things." Philippians 4:8 (ESV)

This is easier said than done. We live in a highly sexualized and elicit culture. Impurity is everywhere. We see it in TV, movies, and best-selling books. Access to pornography is easier than ever before. Children are exposed at a younger and younger age.

Our calling is to live holy lives. Our calling is to be set apart and live different. It is even more critical in this hyper-sexualized world that we strive for purity in our lives.

In 2 Samuel 11:1–27, we read the story of David and Bathsheba. The story begins with David staying behind at the palace while his men went to war. This is the first problem. David was not where he was supposed to be. It left him in a compromising position.

In striving to live pure lives, it is important for us to avoid putting ourselves in compromising positions. This starts with our choices about what we read and what we watch. It starts with what we visit on the Internet. It starts with boundaries we set towards those of the opposite sex.

The second thing that happens is David sees this beautiful woman bathing. But rather than turning away, he inquires as to who she is. Because all the fighting men were at war, there was no one to tell David this was a dumb idea. He had no accountability.

If living pure is a struggle for you, building accountability is one of the most important things you can do. Do you have filters on your computer? Do you have others you can openly talk with about this? Many of us struggle as we fight this battle alone. But this is not a battle to fight alone.

David was the King. He thought he was bigger than this. But this adulterous affair would be his undoing. His family suffered greatly. David would see a daughter raped and sons murdered. All stemmed from this momentary indiscretion. If David had to do it all over again, I am sure he would have run as far as he could run.

> *"Flee from sexual immorality. Every other sin a person commits is outside the body, but the sexually immoral person sins against his own body." 1 Corinthians 6:18 (ESV)*

This verse does not just say avoid sexual immorality. It says flee from sexual immorality. Run away as far as you can. Don't think it could never happen to you. Too many marriages and ministries have been ruined when individuals thought that they were bigger than it.

When we run, God gives us a place to run. We run to Jesus Christ. God created us with a need for him. Jesus is the only thing that will fulfill that need. We try to find fulfillment in so many other things. David had everything as the King, but it still was not enough. He hoped to find in Bathsheba what was missing. What he actually found was that other things in life may satisfy for a short time but never truly satisfy. In the end, he was left with more misery.

It is only in Jesus where we find complete fulfillment. Only he completely fills the emptiness inside. Overcoming impurity is not a matter of will-power, but a matter of God's power at work in you.

13. GIVING UP ENTITLEMENT
Week #2 Wednesday

Scripture Verses

- Mark 10:35–45
- Romans 6:20–23
- Ephesians 2:1–10

Questions to Consider

- What does God owe you? What does the world owe you?
- Why should we be thankful that God does not give to us according to what we are entitled?
- Have you ever been angry with God for not giving you what you wanted?
- How does Jesus help us to overcome our sense of entitlement?

Plan of Action

- Choose to be the servant. Pick one way to serve another person today in an unexpected way.
- Consider something you received which was undeserved. How can you leverage that gift for God's purposes?
- When encountering another person burdened by a sense of entitlement, practice patience and grace. Listen to them. Point them to Jesus by serving them as Jesus serves us.

Reflection

Living with a sense of entitlement makes for a hard life. Yet there are many who walk through life thinking God owes them and the world owes them. When things don't go quite their way, they get upset and they get angry. They live with a bitter heart. Spend a few moments in a customer service department at virtually any store and you will see the sense of entitlement play out.

We see the sense of entitlement play out in our relationships with God. We expect God to give us the job. We expect God to prevent the cancer. We expect God to restore the broken relationship. But then God does not respond in the way we want him to respond.

Have you ever been angry with God? Why? It is anger misdirected. We fail to realize that everything good in our life comes from him. The rest is on us.

The irony is the more we are given, the more our sense of entitlement seems to grow. It is the most privileged that are often the most upset at God. However, the more we are given, the more that is expected of us, not the more we are entitled to receive. With greater privilege comes greater responsibility. When we fail to use our greater privilege for God's kingdom purposes, he will take our privilege and give it to someone else.

God is pouring blessing into our lives. There is nothing we have apart from him. Absolutely nothing! Today the sun comes up. We have eyes to see, mouths to speak, ears to hear, noses to smell, and hands to touch. Every heartbeat is a precious gift. It all comes from him!

Our God is a God of grace. I learned the definition of grace as undeserved love. I have done nothing to deserve anything from him. Everything he gives to me is a free gift. He has been more than kind to me. Anger has no place in my relationship with him. How can I be angry with the one who has given me nothing other than lavish love?

The life Jesus lived for us is the servant life. He doesn't ask for anything but he gives everything.

> *"For even the Son of Man came not to be served but to serve, and to give his life as a ransom for many."*
> *Mark 10:45 (ESV)*

As we follow after him, we strive to follow his example. We may not have much to offer. But what we have, we give to him. That is what worship is. It is trading our attitude "God owes me" with the attitude "I give him everything." In this we honor him, our Servant and Savior, who loves us with an unending love.

14. GIVING UP APATHY
Week #2 Thursday

Scripture Verses

- James 1:26–27
- Matthew 25:31–46
- Luke 7:18–23

Questions to Consider

- What are some of the ways people suffer around the world?
- How does God intend to use you to help them in their need?
- Why are we not more responsive to the needs of others?
- How does God empower us to serve the needs of others?

Plan of Action

- Volunteer to serve with an organization which is working to positively affect the lives of others.
- Be an advocate for others in need. Organize blood drive, food drive, or other type of ministry to help others in need.
- Consider participating in a mission trip to serve others.

Reflection

Most of you who are reading this book are blessed. You eat three full meals a day. You have clean drinking water. You have access to quality medical care. But this is not true for many people living in this world. There is much pain and suffering that goes on.

Diseases of poverty cause 14 million deaths each year. These diseases are caused by contaminated water supply, inadequate sanitation, improper medical care, and poor nutrition. So many of these deaths are preventable.

We might wonder: "Why doesn't someone do something about this?" But the question that comes back to us is: "Why don't we do anything about it?"

There are some reasons why we don't respond to the great need:

Now is not the right time

There is never going to be a good time. There is never going to be enough money. You are never going to be qualified enough. If you are waiting for the perfect time, you will never go. Remember when you are not able, God is more than able.

Someone else will go

We always think someone else is going to go. We think someone else will respond to the crisis. But when God puts a burden upon your heart, recognize it is God calling you to respond. You are God's plan. He has blessed you to make a difference.

It is too overwhelming

There is too much. The challenges around the world are immense. The great need is overwhelming. But God doesn't call you to do it all. He calls you to do your part. He calls you to make a difference one person at a time. That is how it works.

We don't want to go

Does seeing the starving children on TV make you uncomfortable? You are not alone. It is easier to live ignorant of the plight of others. We like it that way. We don't want to see others suffering. It makes us feel guilty. So we go on living busy lives, distracted from the pain around us.

Today, we are going to give up apathy. We are going to care enough to make a difference. When Jesus came to this earth he healed the sick. He made the lame to walk. He gave the blind their sight. He cast out the demons. He offered hope to those without hope. He gave us hope! As we follow him, our Savior, we care because he cared enough for us.

I want to encourage you to get involved making a difference. It may be helping orphans in Haiti. It may be helping provide clean drinking water in Uganda. It may be helping feed children suffering from malnutrition in the Philippines.

The point is God has blessed you. The blessing he gives is not just to be a blessing to yourself, but to be a blessing to others. In Genesis 12:1–3, God told Abram he was going to bless him so that he could be a blessing to others. In 2 Corinthians 1:3–4, it says "God comforts us in our afflictions so that we can comfort others." Do you see it? God helps you, so that you can help others.

You are part of God's plan. It's time to give up apathy and seize his calling. When you follow God's leading, it may end up being one of the most fulfilling things you have ever done. When we hold on to apathy we miss out on so much.

15. GIVING UP HATRED
Week #2 Friday

Scripture Verses

- Psalm 86:1–17
- Matthew 5:38–48
- 1 John 2:7–21

Questions to Consider

- What is hate?
- Where does hate come from? How do we typically respond to hate?
- How do you believe prayer helps transform your hate into love?
- How does Jesus help us to respond to hate with love?

Plan of Action

- Start praying for someone you have feelings of hatred or disgust towards.
- Share with another person about the unconditional love of Jesus.
- Repent of your own hatred and lack of love towards others.

Reflection

Fred Phelps was the founder of Westboro Baptist Church. This church is known for picketing the funerals of dead soldiers. Their message is one of hate. It leaves us to wonder how they could ever consider themselves a church.

When Fred Phelps died, many people celebrated his death. It is easy to join in. Just as this man protested the funerals of so many others, there is a part of us that have liked to have done the same to his. But to have done so would have shown that we are not that much different.

Jesus does not call us to respond to hate with hate. Hatred will destroy us. It will grip us, pull us, and lead us away from Jesus.

Jesus said:

> *"You have heard that it was said, 'You shall love your neighbor and hate your enemy.'" Matthew 5:43 (ESV)*

Hate your enemy! This is the way of the world. This is how the world responds to Fred Phelps. But Jesus goes on to say:

> *"But I say to you, Love your enemies and pray for those who persecute you, so that you may be sons of your Father who is in heaven. For he makes his sun rise on the evil and on the good, and sends rain on the just and on the unjust." Matthew 5:44–45 (ESV)*

This is not easy to do. We can only do this when we are empowered by the love of Jesus. Jesus says to pray for those who persecute you. That is a revolutionary thought. It goes against every natural urge we have.

Prayer has a way of changing the way we think about other people. It's hard to pray for someone and still be hateful towards them. When we start to pray for someone, our hate begins to turn to grief. We grieve over the darkness of their soul. We grieve over the emptiness of their lives. We grieve they miss out on the love of Jesus.

I imagine Fred did not experience much joy in his life. When you are filled with so much hate, there is little room for love. I imagine Fred's life was a very sad life. Even more saddening is that it seems Fred did not know the God of the Bible and the saving grace Jesus offers for sinners. Living apart from God's saving grace leads to an eternity of misery and suffering.

Jesus calls us to live in a different way. This does not mean we honor Fred in his death. We might rejoice in his death, but we will not gloat in his death.

It is ever more important we respond with the love of God and live the love of God. There are other "Fred Phelps" out there who preach hatred in the name of God. If we stay silent about the love of God, how will they ever know anything different.

Martin Luther King, Jr. once said, "Darkness cannot drive out darkness; only light can do that. Hate cannot drive out hate; only love can do that."

It's time to shine the light!

16. GIVING UP NEGATIVITY
Week #2 Saturday

Scripture Verses

- Psalm 46
- 2 Corinthians 4:7–18
- Colossians 3:12–17

Questions to Consider

- How do negative patterns of thought and speech perpetuate themselves?
- What are some things that help you stay positive?
- How does God use negative situations for good?
- How does Jesus give you reason to be positive in the midst of difficult circumstances?

Plan of Action

- If you find yourself stuck in negative patterns of believing and thinking, start a journal. Write each day what you have to be thankful for, what God is teaching you, and ways he is empowering you to serve others.
- Consider putting encouraging Scripture verses in places where you will see them on a regular basis (e.g. fridge, bathroom mirror, computer desktop, car dashboard).
- Smile, sing a song, draw a picture, write some poetry, dance, do something joyful.

Reflection

Are you a glass half empty person? Or are you a glass half full person? What type of person are you?

One thing I have learned is thoughts and words have power. They have more power than we realize. The thoughts of our hearts and the words we choose chart a course. They set us on a path. Those who think and speak in negative ways chart a negative path. Those who think and speak in positive ways chart a positive course.

We all know that person who never seems to be satisfied. They have a way of finding fault in almost every situation. No one ever seems to measure up to their expectations. They are always quick with a complaint or criticism.

The negativity creates a cyclical pattern that builds on itself. Because of the negative energy around that other person, people are less inclined to help that person. People are less inclined to go out of your way for them. As a result, the negative person's negativity is reinforced.

This is not to trivialize or minimize the challenges, hurdles, and obstacles which people face. We can't always choose what happens. Bad things happen in life. There is no doubt we face hardships. There are many situations we encounter that are not positive.

While we can't always choose what happens, we can choose how we respond. The Holy Spirit gives us the ability, through faith, to believe the best and make the most of every situation. With the help of the Holy Spirit, we can develop positive ways of responding to negative situations. The power to respond positively to negative situations starts with our faith in God. Positive people believe the following:

- I believe God has a plan for my life. (see Jeremiah 29:11)
- I believe in God's ability to use other people around me for good. (see Acts 9:26–28)
- I believe God will give me the strength when I need it to overcome the challenges I face. (see Luke 12:12–12)
- I believe God is equipping me through my present challenges to serve him in a greater way. (see 2 Corinthians 12:7–10)

• I believe that while I may be afflicted in every way, I will not be crushed. I may be perplexed, but I will not be driven to despair. I may be persecuted, but I will not be forsaken. I may be struck down, but I will not be destroyed. (see 2 Corinthians 4:8–9)

A powerful lesson I learned is that when something negative happens in your life, the first question to ask is "what does this make possible?" God does not bring the negative events into our lives, but he will open a door through them. Our prayer is God would give us the eyes to see the opportunity he is putting before us.

Keep your head up. Someone once told me that when you have your head down, all you can see is yourself and the challenges you face. But when you look up, you can see God and the possibilities before you.

17. GIVING UP THE SPIRIT OF POVERTY
Week #3 Monday

Scripture Verses

- Matthew 25:14–30
- 2 Corinthians 9:6–15
- Matthew 6:19–24

Questions to Consider

- How is living with a spirit of poverty different from living in poverty?
- Why do we fear there is not enough?
- How is generosity the antidote to the spirit of poverty?
- Why is money one of the truest measures of our trust in God and our understanding of grace?
- How does Jesus help us to overcome a spirit of poverty?

Plan of Action

While not limiting yourself to money, consider one way in the next week you can practice generosity towards:

- Your spouse
- Your children
- Your co-workers
- Your friends
- Your community
- Your church

Reflection

A couple of years ago I took my daughter on a special daddy-daughter date night. Since it was a special evening for my daughter, she got to choose whatever restaurant she wanted. It was not too difficult of a choice for her. She wanted to go to McDonald's and get a Happy Meal.

So we proceeded to the closest McDonald's and I ordered her a Happy Meal. We sat down at our table and began to eat. At one point while we were eating, I asked her if I could have one of her fries. Her response was: "No, mine!"

My thought in that moment was, "who bought you those fries? Who is able to buy you even more fries?" The only reason she had those fries in the first place was because I had bought them for her. What my daughter didn't realize was that I was able to supply her with more fries than she would ever be able to eat. But she was living with a spirit of poverty. Her fear was that she did not have enough fries and would run out. She failed to consider the source of her fries.

That is how it is with God. He gives us everything we have. We don't possess one thing apart from him giving it to us. We may earn our paycheck and buy things with the money we receive. But ultimately it is God who gave us the ability to earn a paycheck in the first place.

Living with a spirit of poverty is not the same thing as living in poverty. Living with a spirit of poverty is living with the fear there is not enough. Living with a spirit of poverty fails to recognize that God is the source of everything we need. The spirit of poverty focuses on what "we can afford" versus what "God can do." We forget God's ability to provide and we limit ourselves to what we can earn.

Many churches are stuck in a spirit of poverty. They forget God is the one who pays the bills. They fear not having enough. The ministry becomes about pinching pennies rather than sowing the seeds of the gospel. When the focus is put on preserving rather than growing, the ministry will become less than effective.

This was why Jesus sent his disciples in Matthew 10:5–15 without anything for the journey. The focus was to rely upon God and know he would provide everything for the journey. If we have God on our side, there is nothing more we need. Effective ministry starts with being faithful to him and trusting in his supply.

The opposite of living with a spirit of poverty is living a generous life. It is living with the mindset that God calls us to use what he has entrusted to us. He calls us not to bury our treasure but to put it to work. If we fail to use what he gives us in ways that he intends us to use it, he will give it to someone else. (see Matthew 25:14–30)

If we want to see a model of generosity, we look to God himself. Jesus our Savior gave us his life upon the cross. We are given the most precious gift of all through Jesus. There is nothing greater he could give. He gave everything. He held nothing back. This is the greatest showing of generosity of all time. If he will give us this greatest gift, is there anything else he would withhold from us for our good and his glory? He has riches in store beyond what we can ever imagine. Every time we take a step of faith to live generously, it builds our trust in his unlimited supply.

18. GIVING UP GOING THROUGH THE MOTIONS
Week #3 Tuesday

Scripture Verses

- Isaiah 1:11–18
- Hosea 6:6
- John 4:20–26

Questions to Consider

- How would you define worship?
- In what ways do you go through the motions of worship? Are there elements of worship you participate in which you don't fully understand?
- What does God desire most in our worship?
- How does a relationship with Jesus affect our worship?

Plan of Action

- If there are any rituals of worship you don't understand, ask your pastor to explain them.
- Examine your calendar and your checkbook. What do these tell you about the gods you serve?
- Consider some ways you might serve God during the week to make your worship on Sunday more meaningful.

Reflection

Worship is about more than going through the motions. We can show up at church each week. We can say all the right things. We can sing all the right songs. We can wear all the right clothes. But it is not worship if Jesus does not live and dwell in our hearts. In other words it is not about right action. It is about a right heart. This is why David writes in the Psalms:

> *"Create in me a clean heart, O God, and renew a right spirit within me." Psalm 51:10 (ESV)*

It is our prayer that our worship would be more than ritualistic expressions void of meaning, but that our worship would come from the heart.

The truest expressions of worship often do not take place within a church building.

Jesus says:

> *"But the hour is coming, and is now here, when the true worshipers will worship the Father in spirit and truth, for the Father is seeking such people to worship him."*
> *John 4:23 (ESV)*

When Jesus originally spoke the words, he spoke them to a Samaritan woman. In the days of Jesus, there was a dispute about the proper place to worship God. The Samaritans said the proper place to worship God was on Mount Gerizim in Samaria. The Jews said the proper place to worship God was on Mount Zion at the Temple in Jerusalem.

Where was the right place? Jesus points out this argument was moot. True worship is not about our physical location. It is about the dwelling place of God in our hearts and lives.

The truest measure of our worship is not what happens on Sunday morning.

The truest measure of our worship is shown at other times through the week. In any given moment, we are worshipping. The question is not if we worship, but what we worship. The gods we worship are shown through the way we invest our time, our money, and our passion. Spend 5 minutes with a person and you can tell a lot about the gods that they serve.

Many of us worship our work. Others of us worship entertainment. Some of us worship sports. A few of us worship our possessions. In what ways do you invest yourself? Who or what is it you serve with your life?

Worship is about what motivates us.

It goes back to our motivation. Who are we doing it for? Many of our expressions of worship come back to ourselves. We see God as a divine vending machine. We put the right things in and we will get the right things out. If we pray the right prayers, attend the right church, and follow all the rules, then God will be good to us. We believe that by doing the right things he will give us full and happy lives.

But our worship must ultimately be motivated by the love of God. Jesus gave us the gift of salvation. We worship him not because of what we might get from him, but because of what he gave us.

Worship is not about what we get, but what we give.

In most churches there is a time for "the offering." But all of worship is an offering. Sometimes we offer our voice in song. Other times we offer our ears to hear his Word.

Beyond the Sunday morning experience, we offer our hands and feet. In the simplest expression, worship is service which is rendered to God and others. We worship God through offering acts of mercy, kindness, and compassion in the name of Jesus.

> *"Truly, I say to you, as you did it to one of the least of these my brothers, you did it to me." Matthew 25:40 (ESV)*

The people who need the love and compassion of Jesus the most are not often found in a church building on a Sunday morning. Motivated by the love of God in our lives, we take our worship beyond the walls of the church building even to places where we might be reluctant to visit. But we go anyway, compelled by our worship of the Savior to shine his light in the darkness. It's time to move beyond going through the motions and live the great adventure!

19. GIVING UP COMPLAINT
Week #3 Wednesday

Scripture Verses

- Jude 17–25
- Psalm 19:1–14
- Exodus 17:1–7

Questions to Consider

- Why do we complain?
- What are the consequences of constant complaining?
- What might you do different when you find yourself overwhelmed by a complaining spirit?
- How does Jesus help us overcome complaining?

Plan of Action

- The opposite of complaint is praise. Go out of your way to intentionally and publicly compliment someone you may not typically praise. Consider someone who might normally be the object of your complaint.
- Give your complaints to God in prayer.
- The next time you find yourself complaining about a situation, ask how you can help to make it better.

Reflection

When our kids start to complain, my wife and I will tell them they sound like Russell from the movie "Up." Maybe you have seen the movie. Russell is a young Wilderness Explorer Scout who is eager to help Mr. Fredericksen, an elderly gentleman (or grumpy old man).

There is one scene in the movie where Russell starts to complain: "I'm tired, my knee hurts … my elbow hurts, and I have to go to the bathroom …"

Are you ever like Russell? We are good at complaining. We complain about the weather. We complain about the traffic. We complain about coworkers. We complain about people at church. There is no limit to the things we are able to find the complain about.

But there is something complaining does to our spirit. It wears us dull. It darkens our soul. It makes us weary.

The weather may be cold. The highways may be congested. Our coworkers may be difficult. The people at church may be hypocritical. But complaining rarely accomplishes anything other than making us feel worse. Instead of complaining, I might offer some other suggestions.

Prayer

We can bear our soul to God in ways we cannot towards other people. The Bible says:

> *"Likewise the Spirit helps us in our weakness. For we do not know what to pray for as we ought, but the Spirit himself intercedes for us with groanings too deep for words." Romans 8:26 (ESV)*

God understands us in a way that no one else can understand. And in those moments where we cannot put words to our thoughts and emotions, the Holy Spirit speaks in our behalf. The other thing about prayer is that prayer works. Complaining does not. When we bring our grievances to the Almighty, he is more than able to respond to our need.

Make a difference

Consider constructive solutions to difficult situations instead of complaining. Consider how you might help the situation. We sometimes fail to realize we are as much of the problem as anyone else. Maybe the reason the situation is like it is, is because no one took the initiative to change it. Many times it is easier for us just to complain about a certain situation than it is for us to take action. So we just complain.

Let it go

Since I already referred to one Disney movie, I will refer to a second. Another favorite movie for our family is "Frozen." We've all heard the song "Let it Go." Sometimes we just need to let it go! You can't change the weather, so why worry about it. It is what it is. Make the most of it. There is a big snow storm bearing down on your town. School is canceled. You can't get to work. Then enjoy the time together with your family.

If we look hard enough, there is something good to be found in every situation. In even the most difficult situations, there is something to be gained. It may be finding a friend who shares a similar struggle. It may be letting go of unrealistic expectations. It may be developing a newfound faith and confidence in God.

Praise

The opposite of complaint is praise. When we speak words of praise it has the opposite effect of when we speak words of complaint. Words of praise uplift our spirits and brighten our souls. Words of praise and affirmation change our outlook. You may not feel it. You might be downcast. But don't let that stop you. Give God the glory. Give him thanks for his goodness. Sing a new song. Then see the new thing God does in you and through you.

20. GIVING UP THE PURSUIT OF HAPPINESS
Week #3 Thursday

Scripture Verses

- Psalm 30:1–12
- Philippians 4:4–7
- James 1:2–4

Questions to Consider

- What makes you happy? What makes you unhappy?
- What is the difference between happiness and joy?
- How do we experience joy even when we may not be happy?
- How does Jesus give us joy?

Plan of Action

- Take a moment and pray to thank God for the moments of happiness in your life. Then ask him for the gift of faith and trust to experience joy in the unhappy moments of life.
- Write down one thing you know will not make you happy, but is the right thing to do. Then go do it. Then come back and write down how God gave you joy in spite of your unhappiness.
- Bring good cheer! Find one way that you can brighten somebody's day. It might be giving a balloon to a child, flowers to a spouse, or a thank you note to a colleague.

Reflection

The Declaration of Independence begins:

"We hold these truths to be self-evident, that all men are created equal, that they are endowed by their Creator with certain unalienable rights, that among these are life, liberty, and the pursuit of happiness."

The pursuit of happiness! It is highlighted in the Declaration of Independence. It was the title of an inspirational movie starring Will Smith. It is what so many people make to be their highest ambition in life.

The pursuit of happiness certainly seems something worthwhile to strive for. It's certainly not a bad thing. It's just not the best thing. Today we will give up the pursuit of happiness in exchange for a fruit of the spirit called "Joy."

Happiness is ever elusive. We take hold of it in a moment. But just as easily as we take hold of it, it slips out of our fingers. Happiness is based upon our circumstances. Some things in life make us happy. Other things make us unhappy. Happiness is temporary because happiness is an emotion based up on our circumstances.

However, joy transcends our circumstances. Joy is a conviction. Joy is developed out of a confident trust in God knowing he is in control and has our best interests at heart. Joy looks beyond our current circumstances to God's ultimate purposes and truths.

If you are married, you know there are moments in life when your spouse makes you happy. You also know there are moments when your spouse does not make you happy. The same is true with our work, school, church, and so many other things in life.

There are many people who think God just wants them to be happy and so they will pursue in any given moment the thing that makes them happy. In the pursuit of happiness, they will exchange the will of God for instant gratification. Happiness becomes a drug that is to be pursued at any cost. It doesn't matter the devastation and the consequences caused in its wake.

Doing the right thing is not always the happy thing. But doing the right thing is ultimately the most fulfilling thing in that it will bring us joy. Joy is about a state of being. It is living with a confident faith and trust in the goodness of God.

The book of Philippians is called a prison epistle. It is a letter written from prison by the Apostle Paul. Prison was certainly not a happy experience for Paul. Ancient prisons would make modern prisons look like the Ritz Carlton. But in spite of apostle's desperate circumstances, he speaks about joy in this letter more than in any of his other writings. He says:

"Rejoice in the Lord always I will say it again rejoice."
Philippians 4:4

It doesn't say rejoice sometimes. It says rejoice always - in the good times and the bad times, the happy times and the unhappy times. Paul could rejoice even in prison because of the relationship he had with God.

So let's give up the pursuit of happiness and join the quest for joy!

21. GIVING UP BITTERNESS
Week #3 Friday

Scripture Verses

- Matthew 6:12–15
- Hebrews 12:12–17
- Luke 15:25–32

Questions to Consider

- What are some reasons people become bitter?
- What are some of the effects of bitterness on people?
- How do you respond when you feel bitterness growing inside you?
- How does Jesus heal us of bitterness?

Plan of Action

- Take a cotton ball and put some vinegar on it. Touch it to your tongue. Consider what the taste of the vinegar tells you about bitterness.
- After tasting of the vinegar, eat some fruit. Consider what the differences are between the vinegar and the fruit. How do the differences relate to bitterness and love?
- Choose love! Release the bitterness you have felt towards a person and ask Jesus for healing.

Reflection

Smoking, drinking, and unhealthy eating are the causes of many illnesses and diseases. But I am more and more convinced that many of our physical maladies are the result of our spiritual condition. Many people carry around bitterness. They are resentful and angry. As the bitterness takes root, it grows within them. Over the days, weeks, and years the bitterness becomes manifested through physical illness and other ailments.

You might be bitter towards a parent or a former spouse. You might be bitter towards a coworker or a supervisor. You might be bitter towards a fellow church member or pastor. But you cannot hold on to the bitterness. The only person your bitterness is hurting is yourself. Bitterness will make you sick. Hebrews 12:17 says:

"The 'root of bitterness' springs up and causes trouble."
Hebrews 12:15 (ESV)

You need to know that bitterness is a tool of the devil. Bitterness destroys relationships. Bitterness locks us in isolation. Bitterness prevents us from experiencing God's healing. We need to strive to release ourselves from the bitterness. Nothing good ever comes from holding on to it. Nothing!

Bitterness is the way of the world. We see bitterness between rival political parties. We see bitterness where there are divisions in the church. We see bitterness between nations. We see bitterness in families. Bitterness seems to be a popular choice we make.

It's not easy to let go - you can't do it on your own. You can only do it through the strength that God gives you through Jesus Christ. I was once told that the person who says forgiveness is easy has never forgiven anyone.

It would have been easy for Jesus to have been bitter. He could have been bitter towards Judas for betraying him. He could have been bitter towards the other disciples for deserting him. He could have been bitter towards the religious leaders for accusing him. He could have been bitter towards the Romans for failing to protect him. He could have been bitter towards us for trivializing his sacrifice. He could have been bitter towards all these people, but instead he chose to die for them.

I find it interesting that he was given the bitter wine vinegar upon the cross to drink (see Matthew 27:48). He physically tasted the bitterness, but bitter was the opposite of what he chose to be. He chose love. Through his blood, he made provision for the forgiveness of all the ways we ever offended him.

Today you may want to be bitter and angry. But let Christ do a new thing in you. Taste of the sweetness of the Gospel!

22. GIVING UP DISTRACTION
Week #3 Saturday

Scripture Verses

- Hebrews 12:1–2
- Mark 1:35
- John 1:14–18

Questions to Consider

- What distracts you from being present with other people around you?
- What distracts you from living out God's agenda for your life?
- What helps you to focus and be the most productive?
- How does Jesus help us focus on what is most important in any given moment?

Plan of Action

- At your next lunch, have everyone set their phone facing down at the middle of the table. The first person who picks up their phone pays for the meal.
- Challenge yourself that the first thing you watch, read, or listen to in the morning when you wake up is God's Word (not email or Facebook).
- Do a digital detox. Turn off everything with a screen for 24 hours. Tomorrow would be a great day to do it, since there is no "40 Things Devotion" on Sunday.

Reflection

We live in an ever connected world. With smart phones at the tip of our fingers, we can instantly communicate with people on the other side of the world. It is an amazing time to live in. I love the possibilities and the opportunities. With the rise of social media, we not only connect with our current circle of friends and family, but we are also able to connect with circles from the past. We can build new communities in the virtual world to find like-minded people we cannot find in our physical world. Services like Facebook, Twitter, YouTube, and Instagram all have tremendous power. They have a way of connecting us with others to shine the light of Jesus.

While all of these wonderful things open up incredible possibilities, there are also many dangers that lurk. One of the biggest dangers is distraction. They keep us from living in the moment and they keep us from enjoying the people sitting right across the room from us. We've all seen that picture where the family is texting one another from across the table. They are not looking at each other. They are looking at the tablet or the phone in front of them. They are distracted in the moment.

Today we are giving up distraction and we are going to live in the moment. Distraction doesn't just come from modern technology. We are distracted by our work. We are distracted by hobbies. We are distracted by entertainment. We are distracted by busyness.

The opposite of distraction is focus. It is setting our hearts and our minds on Jesus. It's not just putting him first. It's about him being a part of everything. It is about making our choices to be God's choices. It is about letting him determine how we use our time and focus our attention. He is the one setting our agenda.

I saw a statistic that 80% of smartphone users will check their phone within the first 15 minutes of waking up. Many of those are checking their phones before they even get out of bed. What are they checking? Social media? Email? The news of the day?

Think about that for a moment. My personal challenge is the first thing I open up every day is God's word. I might open up the Bible on my phone, but I want to make sure the first thing I am looking at is God's agenda. When I open up my email, my mind is quickly set to the tasks those emails generate rather than the tasks God would put before me. Who do I want to set my agenda? For me personally, I know that if God is going to set the agenda, I need to hear from him before I hear from anyone else.

There is a myth called multitasking. We talk about doing it, but it is something impossible to do. We are very good at switching back and forth from different tasks very quickly, but we are never truly doing two things at once. So the challenge is to be present where God has planted you. In any given moment, know what is the one most important thing. Be present in that one thing. Be present here and now.

23. GIVING UP GIVING UP
Week #4 Monday

Scripture Verses

- Romans 12:9–21
- Luke 18:1–8

Questions to Consider

- Are there areas of your life where you felt like giving up on God because he hasn't come through?
- Why do you think God is "slow" to fulfill his promises?
- What does it mean to be persistent with prayer?
- How does Jesus help us to continue to trust in God when we feel like giving up?

Plan of Action

- Make a list of things you wanted, but never got. These are things that now as you look back you are thankful that God didn't answer your prayer in the way you wanted.
- During Lent people practice fasting and deny themselves. One of the things about fasting is that we savor that first meal we partake after the fast. If you fast, think about how enjoyable that next meal is and how much better that meal is because you waited for it.
- God isn't answering something in the way you expect. Start praying on it and start opening the Bible to see what God has to say about it.

Reflection

I am a long-suffering fan of the Chicago Cubs. The Cubs are famous because they have not won a World Series in more than 100 years. I have often been tempted to give up on them. What keeps me going is that I believe this might be the year. They may never win, but I will never give up!

Some of us may feel as if we are long-suffering when it comes to the promises of God. For example, Jesus says:

"I came that they may have life and have it abundantly."
John 10:10 (ESV)

But many of us are experiencing less than that full and abundant life. We have given up hoping for more and we have settled for something less. Maybe you prayed. It didn't work. You went to church. It didn't work. You did everything you could think of, but nothing changed. Rather than thriving, you have settled for surviving.

Jesus tells the story of the persistent widow. She goes to the judge asking for justice. She doesn't get what she asked for. She keeps going back again and again. Finally, she wears the judge down to the point that the judge gives her justice so that she will stop bothering him. Jesus responds to this story by saying:

"And will not God give justice to his elect, who cry to him day and night? Will he delay long over them?"
Luke 18:7 (ESV)

The answer is not so much in us trying more, but in trusting. God keeps all his promises. Maybe not in the way or in the time we expect. There are many things that we don't understand about God. We are told God's ways are higher than our ways and his thoughts are greater than our thoughts (see Isaiah 55:9). We are also told that God is not slow in keeping his promises as some understand slowness (see 2 Peter 3:9). This is where trust comes in. Trust that everything will happen in God's right time (see Galatians 4:4). Trust that he loves you. Trust that he knows what he is doing. Trust that he will respond at the right time.

I don't have all the answers but here are some reasons not to give up on God:

- He is using this time to grow your faith and confidence in him.
- He is using this time to bring you back to him and is waiting for you to call out to him.
- He is teaching you patience.
- He is waiting for you to repent of a persistent sin of which you are currently living unrepentant.
- He wants you to pray.
- He has something better in store that is beyond what you are expecting.
- He is opening a different door of opportunity that you don't yet see because you are not looking for it. You are anticipating God to respond in the way that you expect so you are unable to perceive him responding in a different way.
- There is a step of faith you are not willing to take.

Remember God is God. Those are a few of my thoughts, but my thoughts don't compare to his. So don't give up. Expect more. God is on the move and is able to do immeasurably more than you can imagine (see Ephesians 3:20).

24. GIVING UP MEDIOCRITY
Week #4 Tuesday

Scripture Verses

- Mark 12:41–44
- 1 Timothy 4:6–16
- Deuteronomy 6:4–9

Questions to Consider

- What are the characteristics of an offering (not just money) acceptable to God?
- Why should we strive to give God our best?
- What are some ways to strive to give God our best?
- How does Jesus help us to give God our best?

Plan of Action

- Think about all the ways you serve God. Maybe you play an instrument at your church. Maybe you serve as part of an administrative team. Maybe you volunteer in your local community. What is one way you could improve and grow in your area of service? It might mean reading a book. It could be attending a conference or seminar. It might be taking lesson. If you seek to grow just a little bit each day, it is amazing how much you will grow over time.
- Ask someone to critique your work or service for God. Ask them how you might improve what you are doing. Then listen to them.

Reflection

"In the course of time Cain brought to the LORD an offering of the fruit of the ground, and Abel also brought of the firstborn of his flock and of their fat portions. And the LORD had regard for Abel and his offering, but for Cain and his offering he had no regard. So Cain was very angry, and his face fell." Genesis 4:3–5 (ESV)

Two brothers brought an offering to the Lord. Abel's offering was accepted. Cain's offering was rejected. Able brought the best of his flock. Cain brought something less.

Jesus not only gave it his best, he gave everything. It is our desire to honor him. We don't offer our best to him because our best is required. We offer our best out of love and joy for what he did in our behalf.

Today we are giving up mediocrity. We are giving up on giving God less than our best. We will strive for excellence. It doesn't mean we will always attain it, but excellence is what we will aspire towards.

I live with a holy discontent. The idea is I am never quite satisfied with what I offer to God. Whether it is preaching on a Sunday morning, writing this devotion series, or teaching a Bible study, I am looking for ways to grow and to improve the effectiveness of what I am doing. I certainly find satisfaction in what I offer today, but I am looking for what I can do to make even better what I do tomorrow.

This involves having a teachable spirit. This involves being open to critique and listening to criticism. This is about being humble and recognizing I have room to grow and much to learn. Even though I may be accomplished in a given area, I strive to become more accomplished.

The problem is our fear of critique and criticism. Our pride gets in the way. We fear our areas of growth and improvement are a commentary on our worth and value. To open ourselves up to critique puts us in a vulnerable place. That is not a comfortable place to be and so we close ourselves off to it.

Giving our best is often not about trying harder. It is about being open. It is about listening. It is about humbling ourselves. It is about considering another path and taking a step of faith.

What I offer to God may not be "the best." But I will strive to offer "my best." At the end of the day, I will find satisfaction in that I accomplished all I could for God empowered by the Holy Spirit. I leave with this prayer from God's Word:

> *Let the words of my mouth and the meditation of my heart be acceptable in your sight, O LORD, my rock and my redeemer. Psalm 19:14 (ESV)*

25. GIVING UP DESTRUCTIVE SPEECH
Week #4 Wednesday

Scripture Verses

- James 3:1–12
- Matthew 15:1–11
- Psalm 8:1–9

Questions to Consider

- When have you said something you would rather not have spoken?
- What are the consequences of speaking profanity and other words of impurity?
- How do we tame the tongue?
- How does Jesus help us speak words that are pure and holy?

Plan of Action

- Compliment someone today. Make sure it is sincere.
- Sing a song of praise. Read a psalm of praise. Psalm 8 is a good place to start.
- Eliminate any words from your vocabulary that even hint towards taking the name of God in vain.

Reflection

Do you remember the Smurfs? The Smurfs had a very limited vocabulary. They would smurf every word. They would smurf this and smurf that. Everything was smuf-tastic. Humans have done much the same thing as the Smurfs, but instead of using the word "smurf," humans use words of profanity.

The Wolf of Wall Street set a record for profanity for a US feature film. This movie used a certain profane word 506 times in a span of 180 minutes. The scary thing is that this is not all that surprising when we consider the landscape. Profanity has become a common form of speech. As a father of young children, I am reluctant to take my children to professional sporting events. Even on trips to the local supermarket, you are not sure what you might hear.

But before we are quick to point the finger at others around us, we must be sure to tame our own tongue. The Ten Commandments tell us we are not to take the name of THE LORD our God in vain. Yet, I often hear Christians say, "Oh my God" in very flippant ways. We need to be careful about the context in which we call on God and to hold his name in high regard.

We strive to use God's name in a context of worship. In the Old Testament God was named Yahweh. God's people so revered the name that it was a name that went unspoken. Instead of using the name Yahweh, they would call him Adonai. Adonai is translated "THE LORD." That is why in many Bible translations you will often see "the Lord" written with small capital letters like this: THE LORD. We would do well to hold God's name in a similar regard.

The Bible says:

> *With it (the tongue) we bless our Lord and Father, and with it we curse people who are made in the likeness of God. From the same mouth come blessing and cursing. My brothers, these things ought not to be so.*
> *James 3:1 (ESV)*

Today we strive to tame our tongues. We seek to use our words to be a blessing rather than a curse. This is about more than just purity of speech. This involves the words we speak about others and towards others. These destructive patterns of speech include:

- Gossip - is described in Proverbs 18:8 as delicious morsels that go down in the inner part of the body.
- Innuendo - A close cousin of gossip; to infer something about someone without saying actually saying it.
- Flattery - This is saying to a person's face what you would never say behind their back.
- Criticism - Rejecting others to make us feel good about ourselves.
- Diminishment - A close cousin to criticism, this is when we continually trivialize, minimize, and find fault in another person, effectively demoralizing them.

Words have immense power, more than we realize. James 3:4 likens the tongue to the rudder of a ship, which although small, has the power to turn the ship in any direction. In the previous verse (James 3:3), the tongue is likened to a bit in the mouth of a horse. With the bit in the mouth of the horse, even a 100 pound human can control a 600 pound animal. The point is that our words have power.

As we ponder the sacrifice of Jesus this Lenten season, we realize his name means everything. May our lips speak words which exalt him and build up others.

"O Lord, open my lips, and my mouth will declare your praise." Psalm 51:15 (ESV)

26. GIVING UP BUSYNESS
Week #4 Thursday

Scripture Verses

- Luke 10:38–42
- Matthew 11:25–30

Questions to Consider

- Why do we value busyness?
- How does busyness hinder our relationship with God and others?
- How do we overcome busyness?
- How does Jesus help us overcome busyness?

Plan of Action

- Take a nap. Rest. Relax. Recognize you busyness is only wearing you out.
- Make a check list of the things you need to do. Then set it aside to spend some quality and quantity time with friends and family.
- Give yourself a deadline to get your work done and stick to it. In other words, give yourself a shorter amount of time to get your work done. We typically expand our tasks to the amount of time we allow for them.

Reflection

I love check boxes. I love to-do lists. It feels good when I've got a long to-do list, and I am able to scratch a bunch of things off that list. It leaves me with a sense of accomplishment. I feel good about myself. I like to be busy.

We wear busyness as a badge of honor. We are asked how we are doing and our response is: "Busy!" In our fast-paced culture, we might almost think that there is something wrong if we are not busy. Everyone else is so busy.

But busyness does not always translate to effectiveness. Have you ever had that day when you felt like you were so busy, but wondered what you actually accomplished? Busyness alone does not bear fruit and it is not necessarily what God desires from us. The truth is that our busyness can actually hinder what God wants to do in our lives.

Busyness makes it about what we do rather than about the relationship we have with God. But we love our checkboxes.

❑ Worship on Sunday Morning
❑ Give an offering to the Church
❑ Pray at mealtimes and bed times
❑ Serve in a ministry in the church
❑ Other

We feel as if we can check all the right boxes and then we will be good with God. But imagine if you made your relationship with your spouse about a bunch of checklists. Our spouses are more than boxes to check on our to-do lists. It is the same way with God. We cannot limit him to a checklist.

So let's give up busyness today. In the end, we will discover we spent a lot of time doing things that really did not matter. Let's focus on what most important. In the story of Mary and Martha in Luke 10:38–42, Martha is busy serving Jesus while Mary sits at his feet. Jesus says to Martha:

> *"Martha, Martha, you are anxious and troubled about many things, but one thing is necessary. Mary has chosen the good portion, which will not be taken away from her."*
> *Luke 10:41–42 (ESV)*

Notice Jesus does not say many things are necessary. He says one thing is necessary. So relax. Your busyness for God is not doing anything but wearing you out. God is not counting your checkboxes and neither should you.

Religion is about checkboxes, but Jesus did not come to give us more religion. He came to give us a relationship and rest for our souls!

> *"Take my yoke upon you, and learn from me, for I am gentle and lowly in heart, and you will find rest for your souls. For my yoke is easy, and my burden is light."*
> *Matthew 11:29–30 (ESV)*

27. GIVING UP LONELINESS
Week #4 Friday

Scripture Verses

- Psalm 28:1–9
- Isaiah 53:1–3
- Matthew 28:19–20

Questions to Consider

- What are some of the causes of loneliness?
- Why is it easy to be lonely in the crowd?
- How do you overcome loneliness?
- How does Jesus help us overcome loneliness?

Plan of Action

- Invite a new friend to lunch or dinner. Invite them to play golf or go shopping.
- Next time you are in a large group setting, look for a person who looks awkward or uncomfortable and seek to engage them and learn a little bit about who they are and why they came to the event.
- Make a goal to meet one new person each week before or after worship on a Sunday morning.

Reflection

We have more ways to connect than ever before. We may have hundreds of friends and followers on sites like Facebook and Twitter. But there is an increase in isolation and loneliness. While our relationships may have grown wider, they have often grown more shallow. We have more relationships than ever before, but seemingly fewer meaningful and deep relationships. It's ironic that in a hyper-connected world, loneliness has become an epidemic. We are increasingly isolated from one another. We have become lonely in the crowd.

So today, we are giving up loneliness and isolation. God created us to live in relationship with him. We may be lonely, but we are not alone. God is our first and most important relationship in life. If our relationship with God is right, our other relationships in life will also be right. If our relationship with him is not right, our other relationships in life will not be right. If you have a relationship that you are struggling with, consider what part of your relationship with God might need attention.

When it comes to our relationship with others, recognize God created us as social beings. Companionship is a basic human need. God wired us this way. In the same way, he created us to live in relationship with him - he created us to live in relationship with each other. He did not create us to live separate from one another, but to journey through life together.

Making a friend starts with being a friend. The calling of Jesus is not to wait for someone to befriend us. The calling is to go and be the friend to others. Jesus came as the friend of sinners (Luke 7:34). As we follow in the footsteps of Jesus, we recognize there are many lonely people in need of a friend.

I know there are many introverted people who are reading these devotions. You are uncomfortable engaging with others, but it is time set aside that fear. Any time you are in a group of people, you are certain to find some people who feel uncomfortable, awkward, and out of place. They need a friend. Because of your potential feelings of awkwardness, you just might be the best person to engage them. You can serve them by engaging them and helping to make them feel comfortable.

Are you still afraid? Then ask God to change your heart towards other people. Rather than being worried about their perception of you, ask God to give you a heart to serve them. Stop looking at the situation from the perspective of what other people may think about you. Start with the perspective of God's calling. God's calling is never easy and it is always about loving and serving others. It will lead you to walk across the room and engage others you previously would have ignored. In the process, you discover a new friend. You may be lonely, but you are not alone. God has put people all around you to serve.

28. GIVING UP DISUNITY
Week #5 Saturday

Scripture Verses

- 1 Corinthians 12:12–31
- Ephesians 4:1–16
- John 17:20–26

Questions to Consider

- Where do you see disunity in the world?
- What are the consequences of disunity?
- What is your role as a peace-maker?
- How does Jesus bring peace and reconciliation to a hostile world?

Plan of Action

- What is a sacrifice you need to make for the sake of unity? What are you holding on to out of pride that is hindering unity in your marriage, church, or work?
- Participate in the Lord's Supper this weekend with other brothers and sisters in Christ to find unity with them in Christ's sacrifice.

Reflection

Where there are many visions, there is division. We see it in the politics of America. There are different views about the future of America and how the government should be run. What we are left with is polarization and disunity on many important matters of policy.

We see this same type of disunity within the church. There is competition between denominations. There is competition within denominations. There is also competition within many local churches. Different visions lead to division.

But God does not have multiple visions. He has one vision. His vision is about saving lost sinners. We strive together to seek the implications of this vision in our local context. Maintaining unity is difficult, but here are some important convictions to maintain if we are to stay unified:

Honor those in authority

"Obey your leaders and submit to them, for they are keeping watch over your souls, as those who will have to give an account. Let them do this with joy and not with groaning, for that would be of no advantage to you."
Hebrews 13:17 (ESV)

Whether it is a pastor or a board member, their job is not easy. They have been entrusted with the task to make difficult decisions. We may not always agree with their decisions, but we must honor their decisions and trust they are seeking the Lord. That was why they were appointed to the position they were given.

Celebrate differences

"As it is, there are many parts, yet one body."
1 Corinthians 12:20 (ESV)

Unity is not the same as uniformity. Diversity is something to be celebrated within the church. We look different. We think different. We have different likes and dislikes. We have different gifts. The church would be very boring if everyone was the same.

Differences will sometimes lead to conflict, but we would do well to look for the opportunity in conflict. How do we grow from conflict? What are the lessons to be learned in conflict? How is God refining us during conflict?

Be a peacemaker

Blessed are the peacemakers, for they shall be called sons of God. Matthew 5:9 (ESV)

The amazing thing about God is that he was willing to embrace a humanity which was hostile towards him. To make peace possible, he led with love rather than justice. Rather than holding people accountable for their sins, he sent Jesus. God's love for sinners is relentless.

Like God, we must be willing to lead with love rather than justice. In 2 Corinthians 5:18–19, we are described as ministers of reconciliation. We are agents of peace. We strive for reconciliation by following God's example in that he did not count people's sins against them. He took their sins upon himself. For unity to exist, you must be willing to absorb the sins of others. A peacemaker must be willing to stand in the line of fire and sometimes get burned.

Participation in the Lord's Supper

"For anyone who eats and drinks without discerning the body eats and drinks judgment on himself."
1 Corinthians 11:29 (ESV)

We see the joining of two words in the one word communion (common + union). As the family of God, we hold a unity of faith. We participate in the body and blood of Christ. There is a mystical union. That is what Sacrament is. The Lord's Supper is about more than our relationship with Jesus. There is a reason we receive it together with other believers. Communion is also about our relationship with brothers and sisters in Christ - the body of Christ. Through the Lord's Supper, we are one with Christ, but we are also one with each other. It's the Body of Christ that unites us. I imagine this is one of the reasons Jesus tells us to do this often so that we remember our unity in him.

29. GIVING UP THE QUICK FIX
Week #5 Monday

Scripture Verses

- Hebrews 12:3–17
- Psalm 22:1–31
- Revelation 21:1–8

Questions to Consider

- Is there good to be found in pain?
- In what ways have you been refined through suffering?
- How do you overcome pain (physical, emotional, spiritual) in your life?
- How does God use pain for good? How does he overcome pain?

Plan of Action

- Think about a difficult or hurtful situation in your life. Consider what you can change and do differently. Consider how you are contributing to the hurt.
- Pray! There is no greater gift God gives us when wrestling with pain and suffering. Ask God to reveal what he wants to reveal to you through the pain.

Reflection

It's hard to live with suffering. We do whatever we can to avoid it. And when we encounter suffering, we look for the quick fix. But in our haste to eliminate the pain, we often miss the purpose behind it and the lesson to be learned.

If we have a headache, we take an aspirin. We want pain relief that is quick to eliminate the headache. But in our effort to find the quick fix, we miss discovering the cause behind the pain. The cause of the headache might be dehydration, stress, or lack of sleep. The aspirin is the quick fix, but the real need could be to drink more water, eliminate stress, or get more sleep. When we fail to grasp the root cause of our pain, we will often find ourselves soon experiencing the pain again.

I see this a lot as pastor. A church member comes with a crisis. They want a Bible verse to be read or prayer to be prayed that will make it all better. But sometimes we need to wrestle with God and the cause of our pain. We need to go back to the origins of the pain and our own sin to discover how he is refining us.

The pain tells us something is not right. It gives us the opportunity to discover what needs to change. It points us to find our strength and healing in God. Through the pain we are refined. Through it, God prepares us for future ministry. Through it, we develop greater appreciation for future glory.

Maybe you are struggling in your marriage. You look to read a book on marriage. You go to counseling. You attend a conference. You participate in a couples Bible study. You are looking for that one thing to make everything better. Marriage takes work and effort. There is not a quick fix. A great marriage is not discovered in one thing. Health and healing is approached from all sorts of different angles.

It is true in marriage and in so many other parts of life. Achieving the greatest joys in life is not discovered by following step-by-step instruction manuals. It comes through a lot of hard work, sweat, tears, and faith in God. The greater the struggle while on the journey, the greater appreciation upon reaching the destination.

"It is for discipline that you have to endure. God is treating you as sons. For what son is there whom his father does not discipline?" Hebrews 12:7 (ESV)

I thank God everyday for my experiences in ministry. Some of those experiences I would never want to encounter again. But those experiences formed me into the pastor I am today. They prepared me to accomplish today what I could never have achieved prior to those experiences.

I know God has some great thing in store for your life. It may be difficult right now, but listen to his voice through the pain. Let him refine you and prepare you.

30. GIVING UP WORRY
Week #5 Tuesday

Scripture Verses

- Matthew 6:25–34
- Psalm 46:1–11

Questions to Consider

- Why do we worry?
- What are you worried about?
- How do you overcome worry?
- How does Jesus help you overcome worry?

Plan of Action

- Get to work. When you are busy working towards a solution, it is difficult to find time to worry.
- Journal! This is a great way to collect your thoughts and think through a situation. Sometimes our worry is caused by not adequately assessing a situation.
- Tell God about your worry. Give it to someone who can actually do something about it.

Reflection

Worry does not accomplish anything good. It is not going to help your situation. It is not going to change anything. Jesus himself says:

> *"And which of you by being anxious can add a single hour to his span of life?" Matthew 6:27 (ESV)*

If you are able to accomplish anything through worry, it will not be good. You have heard the saying: "You are going to worry yourself sick." Worry makes you sick. Worry robs you of being healthy, happy, and productive. This is a Biblical principle:

"Anxiety in a man's heart weighs him down, but a good word makes him glad." Proverbs 12:25 (ESV)

Worry is the opposite of trusting God. Worry stems from doubt. It starts when we are unsure of God's providence and plan.

We worry about:

- Things we can't control
- Things we can control
- Things of the past
- Things of the future
- Things known
- Things unknown

There is no end to the things we needlessly worry about. We waste a lot of time and energy worrying about these things. Imagine if the time and energy we spent on worry was applied in a positive way. Many of the things we worry about never actually happen. Worry paralyzes our effectives. It pulls us away from God's path.

The next time you find yourself worrying here are a few ideas:

- **Consider the worst-case scenario.** If you actually considered what the worst-case scenario might be, you may realize it is not all that bad.

- **Do the work.** Do something positive. When you are working towards a solution you have less time to worry. It is when you are not working towards a solution when worry enters the picture. Just tell worry you don't have time.

- **Rebuke it.** Tell your worry it has no place in your life. Tell your worry that you are a child of God and because of that, you have no need for it.

- **Talk to God about it.** The situation and circumstances swirl in our mind all day long. But sometimes you get to the end of the day and you realize you never said anything to God about it.

- **Seek first the kingdom of God and his righteousness. (Matthew 6:33)** When Jesus talks about worry, this is how he tells you to respond. The idea here is to keep seeking. Don't give up. If you are constantly striving for God's will in your life and work, you cannot go wrong. That is not to say it will be easy, but you will be blessed.

31. GIVING UP IDOLIZING
Week #5 Wednesday

Scripture Verses

- Philippians 2:1–11
- Revelation 5:1–14
- Deuteronomy 6:1–9

Questions to Consider

- How is idolatry practiced today?
- What are some idols you make for yourself?
- How do you overcome idolatry?
- How does Jesus conquer idolatry in our lives?

Plan of Action

- Is there another person upon whom you have placed unrealistic expectations? Thank them and encourage them for what they have accomplished even though it did not match what you had expected.
- Under-promise and over-deliver! One of the reasons we disappoint people is because we promise too much. Don't promise what you cannot offer.

Reflection

In the 10 Commandments, we read:

> *"You shall not make for yourself a carved image, or any likeness of anything that is in heaven above, or that is in the earth beneath, or that is in the water under the earth." Exodus 20:4 (ESV)*

In other words, do not make an idol for yourself. In the context of the Old Testament, these idols would come in the form of statutes made of wood or stone. They served a purpose similar to good luck charms. People hoped these idols would bring happiness and prosperity, but God knew that these idols did nothing other than lead people away from trusting in him.

Today we have different idols. We don't often bow down to statues. Our idols come in different forms. Many of our idols come in the form of people. We put them on a pedestal they cannot live up to. Too often we expect more from others than they are able to give. The higher the pedestal we put them on, the further they have to fall.

Recognize that our disappointment in others is often because we are holding them to a higher standard than we hold for ourselves. We are good at practicing forgiveness towards ourselves when we don't meet our expectations. We are not nearly as good practicing that same forgiveness towards others.

Consider some of the ways we unfairly put people on pedestals:

- **We expect them to be gifted in every way.** Sometimes our disappointment is because they cannot deliver in a substantial enough way. Because they are gifted in one way, we assume them to be gifted in another way. People have different ways in which they are gifted. We see this in pastors. Your pastor may be a gifted preacher and teacher. But you get him in a one-on-one situation in a hospital where he does not excel the same way he excels in the pulpit.

- **We expect them to be someone they are not.** Another reason others disappoint us is because they are not the same person we miss or grieve. We talk about someone having big shoes to fill. That new boss is not your previous boss. Don't expect them to be. They are their own person.

- **We expect them to share the same affinities as us.** Another reason people disappoint us is because we expect them to think like us. We expect them to hold the same opinions as us. We expect them to have the same affinities as us. But consider these differences in others to be an opportunity to sharpen us. Iron sharpens iron.

• **We expect them to be perfect and never offend us.** A final reason people disappoint us is we expect them to be without sin. We are somehow surprised when a skeleton is discovered in someone's closet. Consider your own life if you have things you would rather remain hidden. If you do, you are not alone.

This is the reason God says you shall not make an idol. He knows every idol we make will eventually disappoint us. This command is given for our own welfare and benefit. The more we idolize, the harder it is to forgive. The harder it is to forgive, the more weary and burdened our souls will be.

There is only one we worship. There is only one we hold to the highest standard. That is our Savior Jesus. There is truly none like him. He is the only one that will not disappoint.

> *"Therefore God has highly exalted him and bestowed on him the name that is above every name, so that at the name of Jesus every knee should bow, in heaven and on earth and under the earth, and every tongue confess that Jesus Christ is Lord, to the glory of God the Father."*
> *Philippians 2:9–11 (ESV)*

32. GIVING UP RESISTANCE TO CHANGE
Week #5 Thursday

Scripture Verses

- Ecclesiastes 3:1–8
- Matthew 8:24–27

Questions to Consider

- Why is change hard?
- What changes are you resisting that you know you need to make?
- What do you do to embrace change?
- How does Jesus help us change?

Plan of Action

- We become creatures of habit. We fall into certain patterns. Today you are challenged to break a routine. Becoming comfortable changing smaller things helps us become more comfortable when the time comes to change bigger things. This is about training ourselves to become comfortable with change.
- While everything around us changes, you need a solid foundation (see Matthew 8:24–27). Set a certain time of the day for prayer and the study of God's Word. Stick to it. Don't change the time of the day. Don't let anything change this priority. Let that time of the day serve as your anchor.

Reflection

It is said the only thing certain in life is death and taxes. I would suggest another thing which is certain is "change." That's actually the point behind the saying. "Nothing stays the same forever. Seasons come and seasons go" (see Ecclesiastes 3:1–8).

But we resist change. We try as hard as we can to hold on to an ideal past or present. We romanticize about our glory days of the past. We try to keep things the way they are now. But part of the problem with the glory days is they were not as glorious as we make them out to be. The present is not much better. We would do well to envision a changed and better future.

In Matthew 4:12–17, Jesus begins his ministry. The message he preached was:

> **"Repent, for the kingdom of heaven is at hand."**
> **Matthew 4:17 (ESV)**

I want you to pay special attention to that first word which is "Repent." Repent means to turn around and go in a different direction. Repentance is different from confession. Confession is to admit that I am wrong. Repentance is to actually stop what I am doing and to change my ways. Ultimately, repentance is about change in me.

Repentance starts with an open heart. Ask God to reveal in you what needs to be different. Ask him for the desire and the will to make the necessary change. There are many times when we know we need to change, but the change we need to make is just too hard. Rely upon his strength!

One of the keys to embracing the necessary change is having a solid foundation. If you have a solid foundation, change is not something to be feared. For us, our solid foundation is Jesus. He keeps us centered and secure. The Bible tells us:

> **"Jesus Christ is the same yesterday and today and forever." Hebrews 13:8 (ESV)**

He is the Alpha and the Omega. He is the beginning and the end. He is the most certain thing we have in life. When our world is rocked, he doesn't roll away.

There is also the change around us. That change will often come like a tsunami and there is no way to stand against that wave. We have seen sweeping changes over the landscape of America and the social climate. There are numerous approaches people take in regards to the change. Some will fight it. Some will bury their heads in the sand. Still others embrace it.

I may not always like what is happening around me. I may be upset about what is changing. I have found that when I am uncomfortable with the changes around me, it is time to go back to God and ask him what he wants to change in me. The problem is not always with what is happening around me, but the problem is often with what is happening in my heart. The world is changing everyday. If you allow God to change you and mold you, the future is full of exciting possibilities.

> *"But now, O LORD, you are our Father; we are the clay, and you are our potter; we are all the work of your hand."*
> *Isaiah 64:8 (ESV)*

33. GIVING UP PRIDE
Week #5 Friday

Scripture Verses

- Psalm 51:17
- Micah 6:6–8
- Matthew 23:1–12

Questions to Consider

- What does it mean to be humble?
- From what areas of your life do you need to eliminate pride?
- How do you practice humility?
- How does Jesus give us humility?

Plan of Action

- The next time you pray, really get on your knees. We talk and sing about bowing before God, but we don't often do it. We most often sit or stand to pray. Consider actually humbling yourself and to truly bow before him.
- A humble spirit is one that is willing to give others credit and rejoice when others are lifted up. Make a point to offer praise to others for what God is accomplishing through them. Do it today!

Reflection

> *"Humble yourselves before the Lord, and he will exalt you." James 4:10 (ESV)*

Pride keeps us from experiencing the abundance of God. Pride puts a wall between us and him.

It was because of pride, Satan was cast from heaven as a fallen angel. His entire nature is pride. He spews his poison through lies to the ends of the earth. When we go back to the original sin in the Garden of Eden. The serpent said to Eve:

"For God knows that when you eat of it your eyes will be opened, and you will be like God, knowing good and evil." *Genesis 3:5 (ESV)*

"You will be like God!" As Eve listened to the twisted truth of the serpent, she yielded her desire to serve God in exchange for the idea of becoming God. As she bit of the fruit, the poison of pride entered her soul. She became corrupted with the pride of the serpent. Lost was the humble dependence upon God which provided abundant and eternal life. Up to this point only good was known. Now humanity would know not only the goodness of God but also the evil caused by pride.

Pride is about putting ourselves in the place of God. Much of the sin and hardship in our lives goes back to pride. We get ourselves into trouble when we begin to think we know better than God. We make the "Ten Commandments" into "Ten Suggestions" and go our own way.

The picture at the end of the Bible in Revelation is a picture of true humility restored before God. The Elders bow down and cast their crowns before the throne and worship him saying:

"Worthy are you, our Lord and God, To receive glory and honor and power, For you created all things, And by your will they existed and were created." Revelation 4:11 (ESV)

We learn humility and receive from Jesus. The chief characteristic of Jesus is one of humility:

• He humbled himself by taking on human flesh.
• He humbled himself by associating himself with sinners.
• He humbled himself by becoming a servant.
• He humbled himself to be arrested and to be judged by human

authority.

- He humbled himself through his agonizing death on the cross.
- He humbled himself in that he became sin who knew no sin.

But the humility of Jesus is not the end of the story. It was God the Father who exalted him:

- He was exalted in that he rose from the dead.
- He was exalted in that he ascended into heaven.
- He is exalted that now he sits on the right hand of the throne of God.
- He is exalted that he will come to judge the living and the dead.
- He is exalted that every knee will bow and every tongue will confess he is Lord.

Who sits on the throne in your life? Who makes the decisions? Humility starts with giving the lordship of your life over to Jesus. It's casting your crown before him and saying: "I don't want this or need this. It is your's Jesus!"

In the end, humility puts us in a place to receive God's abundant grace. It also puts us in a place to be used by him in powerful and amazing ways.

"Blessed are the meek, for they shall inherit the earth." Matthew 5:5 (ESV)

34. GIVING UP
A SMALL VIEW OF GOD
Week #5 Saturday

Scripture Verses

- Psalm 19:1–14
- Genesis 1:1–31
- Ephesians 3:14–19

Questions to Consider

- What does creation tell us about God?
- Why do we put limits on the glory and power of God?
- How does seeing God for who he is, give us confidence in the face of trial and adversity?
- What does it mean to you that the God of the universe wants to have a relationship with you?

Plan of Action

- Go outside at night and look up. Consider the vastness of the universe and what it took to create it. Thank God for how amazing he is.
- The next time you are feeling overwhelmed by a problem, read Psalm 19 and consider the universe.

Reflection

I've always been fascinated with astronomy. To me, astronomy is the study of just how big our God is. The study of astronomy is something so humbling. If you want to feel small, just look at the sky.

It says in the Psalms:

> **_"The heavens declare the glory of God, and the sky above proclaims his handiwork." Psalm 19:1 (ESV)_**

In 1990, the Spacecraft Voyager reached the edge of the solar system after traveling for 12 years at a speed of 40,000 miles per hour. Scientists told the spacecraft to turn around and take a picture where it came from. You can find this picture if you google: Pale Blue Dot.

The picture looks like someone forgot to take the lens cap off the camera. But the reality is that this is the darkness of space. The muted rays of color in the picture and these are rays of the sun reflecting off the spacecraft. If you look closely enough at the picture, you will see in a beam of light one small white pixel that looks out of place. It's a picture of you! Did you smile? That one small white pixel is the Earth.

Are you feeling small? If not, consider this: Light travels at 186,000 miles/second. That is really fast. What that means is that it takes one second for light to travel 7.5 times around the earth. It takes 8 minutes and 17 seconds to get here from the sun 93 million miles away.

The reason I talk about the speed of light is because the mile is a useless measurement in space. When we start talking about space, we use the measurement of the light year. Light will travel 5.9 trillion miles in one year. Some implications of this:

- Realize that it would take more than 4 light years to reach the next closest star beyond our sun. There is no technology available today that would even allow us to consider making it there.
- Even if we could travel at the speed of light, we could not travel across our galaxy in our lifetime. It is estimated our Milky Way Galaxy would take 100,000 years to travel across at the speed of light. And to think there are many more galaxies beyond our own Milky Way Galaxy.

- The next closest galaxy, Andromeda, is is 2.2 million light years away. If you are wondering, we are scheduled to collide with Andromeda in 5 billion years.

In so many ways, the universe is bigger than our reach and our understanding. This is not so much an exercise to make you feel small, but to help you realize just how big God is. When we think about God, he is bigger than the universe. He created it. He formed the sun, the Milky Way, and the other distant galaxies in the universe.

It has been said, "don't tell your God how big your problem is, tell your problem how big your God is." It is amazing to think how the God of the infinite universe cares about you so much that he knows even the number of hairs on your head. He is your creator and he knows you even better than you know yourself. So let's give up our small view of God!

35. GIVING UP ENVY
Holy Week Monday

Scripture Verses

- Psalm 37:1–40
- 1 Corinthians 3:1–15

Questions to Consider

- What do you envy in others?
- What are the consequences of envy?
- How do you overcome envy? What is the opposite of envy?
- How is Jesus the answer to envy?

Plan of Action

- Overcoming envy involves being grateful for what God gives us. You have been blessed in ways that others are not. Make a list of special blessings God has put in your life.
- We might describe envy as misplaced zeal. What are you zealous for? Do you have a personal life vision or calling that God has placed upon you? If not, take some time today to write it out. Victory over envy starts with having a clear life purpose and knowing what God gives you to accomplish it.

Reflection

Envy is an overwhelming desire to possess what others have. Envy takes many forms. We become envious of others for their position, accomplishments, social standing, and material possessions. Envy causes us to despise rather than rejoice in the good fortune of others.

Nothing good comes from envy. Envy leads to sorrow. It leaves us with an empty feeling and a hole in our heart. In many cases, it will even lead to greater misfortune. This was the case with King Saul in ancient Israel. After David defeated Goliath, we read how Saul grew envious of David:

> *"As they were coming home, when David returned from striking down the Philistine, the women came out of all the cities of Israel, singing and dancing, to meet King Saul, with tambourines, with songs of joy, and with musical instruments. And the women sang to one another as they celebrated, "Saul has struck down his thousands, and David his ten thousands." And Saul was very angry, and this saying displeased him. He said, "They have ascribed to David ten thousands, and to me they have ascribed thousands, and what more can he have but the kingdom?" And Saul eyed David from that day on."*
>
> *1 Samuel 18:6–9 (ESV)*

Saul became envious of David for the praise David received. The real enemy was the Philistines, but envy caused Saul to make David into an enemy. David had defended the nation against the Philistines by defeating the Philistine champion. He was one of Saul's greatest assets. But Saul despised the fact that David received greater praise.

Saul became intent on having David killed. Instead of using the military to protect against the Philistines, Saul used the military to pursue David. This became a major liability. It left Saul and his army vulnerable against the Philistines. Eventually, Saul was killed in a battle against the Philistines. It leaves one to wonder what would have happened if Saul had not been so envious of David. What would have happened if Saul had befriended David and used David to fight the real enemy?

Envy causes us to loose sight of the real enemy. We let our guard down and we are left vulnerable to the enemy. Envy makes us blind to the goodness of God in our life because we are consumed with what we don't have.

It was out of envy that Jesus was handed over to the Romans to be crucified (see Matthew 27:18). The religious leaders were envious of how the people were following Jesus. They saw Jesus as a threat to their power and prestige. They would not rest until they had Jesus crucified. Because of envy, they missed what God was doing. Rather than partnering with God on his mission, envy left them fighting against God. It was not a winning proposition.

Envy caused the religious leaders to despise God's greatest blessing. Jesus was not one to envy, but one to embrace. The point is not to let envy blind you to the blessings God is pouring into your life. What person have you become envious of that God is calling you to embrace rather than despise?

God has placed a calling on your life. You have everything you need. More than you realize! Many times God provides for us through other people. They will be blessed in ways that you are not. At the same time you are blessed in ways they are not. Live with zeal for the mission of God. He will bring gifted people into your life to accomplish more than you ever imagined possible.

36. GIVING UP UNGRATEFULNESS
Holy Week Tuesday

Scripture Verses

- Psalm 100:1–5
- Psalm 118:1–29
- Luke 17:11–19
- 1 Thessalonians 5:16–19

Questions to Consider

- What do you have to be thankful for?
- What causes us to be ungrateful?
- How do you cultivate a grateful heart?
- How does Jesus create gratefulness within us?

Plan of Action

- Listen to positive and uplifting music. It does our soul good and helps cultivate gratitude in our heart. Another thing you might consider is rc-reading the Psalms above. Remember the Psalms are songs.
- Make a list of all the things Jesus means to you.
- Express your gratitude. Share with others what you are thankful for.

Reflection

Every year in the United States, we set aside the fourth Thursday in November to give thanks for all our blessings. It is a beautiful day. It is a day to enjoy being together with family. The turkey is carved. There is no need to exchange gifts, because the focus is on all that we have already been given.

Then the next day we scratch, claw, and fight in the shopping malls for all the things we don't have. We see people trampling over other people in department stores to get the great deal. Have you ever caught the irony of this? One day is all about the things God has poured into our lives. The next day is about all the things we are lacking.

Gratitude is not something that can be manufactured. Setting aside at day to be thankful is not going to automatically make us grateful.

Another trick we use to try to manufacture gratitude is to compare ourselves to others less fortunate. Maybe you have seen this list which has circulated on the internet the last few years:

- If you have food in your fridge, clothes on your back, a roof over your head and a place to sleep you are richer than 75% of the world.
- If you have money in the bank, your wallet, and some spare change you are among the top 8% of the world's wealthy.
- If you woke up this morning with more health than illness you are more blessed than the million people who will not survive this week.
- If you have never experienced the danger of battle, the agony of imprisonment or torture, or the horrible pangs of starvation you are luckier than 500 million people alive and suffering.
- If you can read this message you are more fortunate than 3 billion people in the world who cannot read it at all.

Gratitude cannot be manufactured by guilt. We might think that the more we have, the more thankful we will be. But those who are given more are often the least grateful. Those with less are often the most grateful. It is backwards from the way that we think it should be.

In Luke 17:11–19 Jesus heals 10 lepers of their disease. After they are healed, only one returns to thank Jesus for what he had done. You might have thought that all 10 would have been thankful for the incredible gift they received. It's just not the way that it works.

Gratitude cannot be measured by the amount of blessing poured into our lives. Gratitude is a heart matter. What is in our heart will come out. Is your heart's desire for Jesus or is your heart's desire for more stuff? If Jesus is truly our heart's desire, then we will have all we need and more. Ask Jesus to come and dwell in you richly so you might give him thanks with a grateful heart.

37. GIVING UP SELFISH AMBITION
Holy Week Wednesday

Scripture Verses

- Philippians 3:4–11
- Genesis 11:1–9
- Ecclesiastes 1:1–11

Questions to Consider

- Why is selfish ambition so attractive?
- What are the consequences of selfish ambition?
- How do you overcome selfish ambition?
- How does Christ conquer selfish ambition?

Plan of Action

- Make a list of the ways you see God moving and working around you. Then consider how you might join in.
- Be a part of something bigger than yourself. God's vision is always bigger than you. I was told as a young pastor to never do ministry alone. If you are doing all the work yourself, then it probably is not God's work. God's mission is a mission to share.

Reflection

You have been told that you can do it if you set your mind to it. If you work hard enough and have enough ingenuity, creativity, and imagination, the sky is the limit. Nothing is impossible. You can do it. This is at the very fabric of the American Dream. The American

Dream is about becoming a self-made man or woman. Our nation was founded as the land of opportunity. It was a place that through hard work and ingenuity you had the freedom to achieve your dream.

This all sounds great. However, we must be careful to tread lightly here. There are subtle dangers which lurk. Such talk easily sets us up for disillusionment and worse. While there are many great success stories, there are also stories of epic failures. As much as I desired to become a professional baseball player and lead the Chicago Cubs to their first World Series in over 100 years, it never happened. Our dreams don't always work out. Sometimes we are left on the outside looking in.

Another danger is that we replace God's desire for us with "our American Dream." Our American Dream becomes about bringing attention to our accomplishments. We want the big house, not because we necessarily need the big house. We want the fancy car, not because we need the fancy car. We want them because they are status symbols. They show others that we have made it. They show off how successful we have become. Dave Ramsey puts it into context. He says:

> *"We buy things we don't need with money we don't have to impress people we don't like."*

"Our American Dream" easily becomes a new religion we passionately pursue. In this new religion, God becomes a means to an end. He is there to help us accomplish our dream and the god we worship is ourselves. Our mission is not about accomplishing God's dream, but accomplishing our dream.

There are many Bible verses that talk about how we can do all things and how we can ask for whatever we want and it will be given us. These are promises, but we need to remember the premises that come before the promises. We need to remember what the promises are about.

The promises of God are about him

We make our strategic plans. We set our agenda. We develop our priorities. We identify our goals and objectives. Then after all that is done, we ask God to come alongside us and bless us.

But what if the starting point was God's plans? Consider what God is doing and how he is moving. Take a few moments and consider where God is at work. Write it down. As you consider where God is at work, ask yourself how you can join him and be a part of what he is already doing. This is not about asking God to come alongside of us. This is about coming alongside God where he is already at work.

The promises of God are about the community

Many of the promises in Scripture are not given to individuals, but to the community. The translation of Matthew 6:33 reads: "Seek first the kingdom of God and his righteousness and all these things will be given to you as well." What a great promise that all things will be given. But don't miss the premise with the promise. An accurate translation is not "You (singular) seek first the kingdom." The translation is properly rendered "You (all) seek first the kingdom." The promise is given to the community called the church as it collectively pursues God's mission.

The promises of God are about his mission

Another thing about the premises to the promise is they are focused on overcoming for the sake of God's mission. In Philippians 4:13 Paul talks about how he can do all things through Christ who strengthens him. But he really was not talking about accomplishing ambitious dreams or goals he had set. At the time, he was in prison because of his preaching of the gospel. His reference was that he could endure his prison sentence, which was a result of the calling placed on his life.

The American Dream seems very appealing, but as we dig deeper we will discover that God's Dream will trump the American Dream every time. We discover that all our accomplishments in this world don't really amount to very much. In comparison, Jesus has accomplished immeasurably more than we could ever imagine. There is nothing greater we can draw attention to than to draw attention to Jesus.

38. GIVING UP SELF-SUFFICIENCY
Maundy Thursday

Scripture Verses

- Matthew 26:14–75

Questions to Consider

- Why do we have difficulty asking for help?
- What is wrong with not asking for help?
- What is the proper way to ask for help? From others? From God?
- How does God offer us help?

Plan of Action

- Ask for help.
- Find a prayer partner. Ask them to pray for you personally. Share with them things you are personally struggling with.
- Participate with God's family in Maundy Thursday Worship.

Reflection

Today is Maundy Thursday. It was on this day that Jesus shared the Last Supper with his disciples. This was an extremely difficult day for Jesus. Everything was coming to a head. He was betrayed by Judas, abandoned by the disciples, arrested in the Garden of Gethsemane, denied by Peter, and put on trial before the religious leaders.

In agony, he prayed that night, "Father, take this cup of suffering from me." As he prayed, his sweat became drops of blood. The weight of the world was bearing down on him. It was a cry of distress.

There are times when it seems the weight of the world comes crashing down on us. Other times we may not feel such tremendous weight, but at any given time we are bearing certain hurts, struggles, and trials we are going through. Yet many times we play a game and pretend that everything is okay. We are asked how we are doing and we responded by saying: "good." We want to present the perfect "Christmas card picture" with the happy family where life is great.

As a pastor, I will often ask people how I can pray for them. Most often the response I get is a request to pray for friends and family members. Their brother is sick, their co-worker lost their mother, or a friend is going through a divorce. It was much rarer for someone to actually request prayer for themselves.

We take the attitude that I'm okay and you're okay. But the truth is that not everything is okay. We have difficulty asking for help. We pride ourselves in our self-sufficiency. We fear that by asking for help we are somehow less of a person. We fear being made into a "charity case."

The truth is that we are all charity cases. The Biblical Greek word for grace is "charis" from which we get the word charity. Grace is charity and it is through grace that God helps us in our need. We have a sin problem and thanks be to God we receive our help through Jesus Christ.

It is time to give up self-sufficiency. Know that it is better than okay to ask for help. We need help. God gave us each other to help each other out. This design goes all the way back to Genesis. God first created man. The next person he created was woman. She was described as a helper. This is why God gives us other people. They are there to help us out.

It can be difficult to admit needing help, but I have found it extremely rewarding. Not only are other people more than willing to help, but oftentimes they begin to open up about how they need help. Being part of a supportive community is so much better than the masquerading community where everyone and everything is okay. It is a beautiful thing to be a part of a community where individuals are willing to make themselves vulnerable to ask for support and then to have such support offered and received.

Just to conclude, I want to say thanks to everyone who has helped me out! Love you all.

39. GIVING UP SORROW
Good Friday

Scripture Verses

- Matthew 27:1–66
- 1 Corinthians 15:1–58

Questions to Consider

- Why is Good Friday good?
- Why should we not fear death?
- What does it mean that Jesus conquered death?

Plan of Action

- Remember the cross and the resurrection. Simply reflect upon the implications of the above readings.
- Participate in Good Friday Worship

Reflection

What is so good about Friday? Jesus died. It was a day of darkness, agony, and suffering. On this day, many of us will participate in worship which is somber and sorrowful. It doesn't seem so good.

This world is filled with grief. There is not a single person reading this who has not been touched by death in someway. There is pain and it endures a lifetime. While we may experience some healing from the pain of the loss, we will never be the same in this lifetime. There is part of us missing. It doesn't seem so good.

Not only do we experience the pain of sorrow when it comes to death, we are also confronted with our own mortality. Our time on this earth is short. With the exception of Enoch and Elijah, the mortality rate is 100%. Sin has rendered us all with a terminal diagnosis. It's not if we will die, but when we will die. It doesn't seem so good.

It certainly doesn't seem so good, but the reason we call Good Friday "good" is that it is not the end of the story. Sorrow does not get the last laugh. It may be Friday but Sunday is coming. There is more of the story yet to be told. The final act has yet to play out.

The Apostle Paul writes:

> *"But we do not want you to be uninformed, brothers, about those who are asleep, that you may not grieve as others do who have no hope." 1 Thessalonians 4:13 (ESV)*

He does not say we do not grieve. Yes, we grieve. We grieve because of the reality of death we are confronted with. There are tears to be shed as long as we walk this earth, but we do not grieve as those who are without hope.

You might have been told to never put a period where a comma belongs. For those of us who are believers, death is not the period. It is the comma. Death is not good-bye. It is see-you-later.

On Sunday, we celebrate the resurrection. Without Sunday, there is no "good" in Friday. The resurrection gives us the conviction to say:

> *"O death, where is your victory? O death, where is your sting?" 1 Corinthians 15:55 (ESV)*

Jesus makes possible a new order. Death is a doorway to a new and blessed life.

> *"He will wipe away every tear from their eyes, and death shall be no more, neither shall there be mourning, nor crying, nor pain anymore, for the former things have passed away." Revelation 21:4 (ESV)*

On this Good Friday, we remember the saving work of Jesus upon the cross. It is finished! The cross is behind us. It is "good" because Jesus is risen just as he said. It's okay to shed a tear today, but make sure to mix joy with the sorrow.

40. GIVING UP MY LIFE
Holy Saturday

Scripture Verses

- Matthew 28:1–10
- Matthew 16:24–28

Questions to Consider

- Why are we reluctant to give everything to God?
- What does it mean to give your life to God?
- What enables you to give God your life?
- Why did Jesus give us everything?

Plan of Action

- What has God given you that you could use to bless and serve others? Take one possession, ability, or gift and consecrate it to God's purposes.
- Celebrate the resurrection by participating in Easter Sunday Worship.

Reflection

We have given up many things over the last 40 days of Lent, but on this final day we are giving up everything. We give our lives to the one who created us, saved us from our sin, and is coming to take us home. We surrender all to him who gave all.

He is our maker and owner. Everything we possess is already his. The money in our pockets is not our possession. None of our possessions do we really own. We brought none of this into the world and we are not going to be taking any of it with us. It is simply on loan to us while we walk this earth.

Neither are our bodies our own. God gives us these bodies to live in while we are here. But in the resurrection, we are given new spiritual bodies not like the bodies we live in now (see 1 Corinthians 15:44).

Our children are not our own. They are God's children. They belong to him, but he has entrusted us with them to raise and nurture in the faith. This is an incredible responsibility he assigns us.

The point of all this is that we are God's servants. He is the master. We are stewards and managers of all that he possesses. Nothing is ours. This is our Father's world. In the end, we will give an accounting for what we did with all that he entrusted to us. I know that my prayer is I will hear the words, "well done good and faithful servant."

Think about the delivery man. You are the owner of the package and you entrust the delivery man to deliver the package to the destination you intend. If that delivery man was to take your package to his home for himself, you would consider that theft. It is theft because he is not the owner of the package. He is just a steward of the package.

We are not much different from the thieving delivery man when we use what God entrusts to us in ways God did not intend for us to use it. We talk about tithing God the first 10% of our income. At that point, we think we have done our job. But that first 10% is just the start. We also seek to use the other 90% in a way he intends. He gives the rest of it to us to provide for our basic needs, to serve others, and to bring him glory.

The more we are given the more that is expected of us. Jesus says:

> *"Everyone to whom much was given, of him much will be required, and from him to whom they entrusted much, they will demand the more." Luke 12:48 (ESV)*

It's not just about our money. It is our time. It is the gifts and abilities we possess. It is every breath we breathe. It is every beat of our hearts. May they all be used to honor him our Lord of lords and King of kings!

Take my life, and let it be consecrated, Lord, to Thee.
Take my moments and my days; let them flow in ceaseless praise.
Take my hands, and let them move at the impulse of Thy love.
Take my feet, and let them be swift and beautiful for Thee.

CONCLUSION

As we have come to the end of this devotion series, I wanted to share a little about the genesis of the 40 Things to Give up for Lent.

I had served as the Pastor of Lutheran Church of the Good Shepherd for about 10 months. Good Shepherd (gs4nj.org) is a small church. Average attendance on Sunday morning is about 135. God has blessed our church and we have grown over time. One of the things we continue to pray for is that God would continue to grow our church and fill the empty pews on Sunday morning. But we have learned that when we pray for something, God often has something bigger in mind. We didn't have nearly enough pews to accommodate everyone who would be impacted by our ministry through 40 Things.

The Commitment

As we approached the season of Lent, I began to pray and consider some ways I might meaningfully observe this season of the church year. I had long had a blog, but only occasionally posted. I had never put much effort into it. As I prayed over all this, I felt God was leading me to share what I was learning. Certainly I shared what I was learning through the sermons I preached and the Bible Studies I taught, but I believed the blog was another avenue to be used. So I made a commitment to God and myself to blog everyday about what I was learning during the season of Lent.

At first, I thought I would use the Good Shepherd Daily Bible Readings as the inspiration for my posts. I typically write something everyday on these readings, but I keep my writings in a personal journal. The difference now was I would make a concerted effort to share what I was writing with others. Writing is the easy part. The more difficult part for me was actually sharing. But I prayed to God that if he gave me the words, I would share what gave me. While I thought the daily Bible readings would be the inspiration, I would soon discover God would give me some new inspiration.

The Viral Post

All this took place a week and a half before Lent 2014 when I made that commitment. I was not sure anyone would take the time to read what I was going to share. But that really did not matter. Ultimately, this was about my own personal journey. If someone else was blessed by what I would share, then great. So I started to write daily on my blog in anticipation of Lent.

Like most weeks I sat down to pray and write my weekly email newsletter article to the members of Good Shepherd. The topic of the week was going to be on Lent which was a week away. We had Ash Wednesday worship coming up. I also wanted to talk some about how people were preparing to observe Lent. I knew that many people traditionally give something up for Lent. So I wanted to speak to that, but put a new twist on it. I ended up writing the original article entitled 20 Things to Give up for Lent.

The topic was something which had been swirling around in my mind for some time. I cranked out the article in about 10 minutes and posted it on our church website. I did all the normal things I do. I posted it on Facebook and Twitter and scheduled the weekly email to go out the next day. The article was posted on the website on Thursday. The email went out on Friday.

As a small local church our website would generally see about 40 people logging in each day. On the days of the week I would send out my email, we might have 120 hits. On a really good day, we might surpass 200 people checking things out.

On the Thursday I posted the article, our website hit 404 visitors. All these visitors on Thursday came mostly via Facebook as the weekly email had not yet gone out. I knew then that this post had struck a nerve. After the weekly email went out, our website generated 644 visitors on Friday. This was all very exciting, but this was just the beginning.

The weekend came and on Saturday the momentum really started to build. 5,523 visitors came on to the site. This was a new record for our website. There was a lot of buzz on Facebook. People were starting to comment on the site. Sunday came and on this day we had 35,973 visitors on the site. The momentum continued building.

The weekend came to a close. The beginning of the work week came and this was when everything went wild. Monday saw more than 280,000 visitors to the site. We had emails and phone calls coming into the church at an incredible pace from all around the world. I stood in amazement at all this. Over the course of the week, we had more than one million visits to our website. This happened in spite of the fact that our hosted website crashed several times on the busiest two days.

Following God's lead

God had given me what he wanted me to write about during the season of Lent. I had made the commitment to write something every day and he had showed me a subject which had struck a nerve. For the 40 Days of Lent I blogged a devotion series called the 40 Things to Give up for Lent. We had more than 10,000 people sign up to receive these posts via email each day.

We heard back from people all over the world how instrumental and transformational these devotions were. Several people reached out for help and support for various challenges they are facing. It was a privilege to help minister to them and pray with them.

This devotion book that you are reading is the compilation of the 40 Things to Give up for Lent devotion series. After the tremendous response, we wanted to be able to share it with even more people.

Lessons Learned

The reason I write this is I believe it is important to keep a record of God's faithfulness. This is an opportunity to reflect on lessons learned. So here are a couple lessons I learned:

• God honors commitments made to him. When you make a commitment to serve him and others, he will prosper the commitment. The problem is the commitments we make are often centered on ourselves rather than on him.

• Come alongside what God is blessing. Sometimes we focus on strategic planning. We make our plans and then ask God if he will be a part of those plans. There was no strategic plan here. It was just simply following God where he was leading and watching to see the doors he was opening up.

• There are no coincidences. Instead of coincidences, we will call them God incidents. I will not go into everything here, but all the pieces were in place to make this happen.

• There is a hunger and thirst for Jesus. There is much said and written about the decline of "religion" in America. But someone once told me that there is a God-sized hole in every person's heart. Only God can fill that hole. We can't fill that hole with religion. It is only a relationship with Jesus that satisfies. I attribute the amazing response to this series to the great desire to find the hope that is only offered in Jesus. We must move past the trappings of religion and point to Jesus.

• Share what you are learning with others. God blesses you so that you can be a blessing to others. Do you want to learn something well? Then start teaching it! You will be amazed how people respond.

• God answers prayer. I already knew that, but every time I see him come through it gives me even greater assurance.

I pray you have been blessed through the resources we have been able to offer. We would love to hear how the 40 Things to Give up for Lent has touched you or blessed you.

God's blessings,

Pastor Phil
phil@gs4nj.org

Made in the USA
Middletown, DE
26 February 2017